COLLINS PHRASE BOOKS

SPANISH

Compiled by

Edwin Carpenter
with
Isabel Carrera

COLLINS
LONDON & GLASGOW

First Published 1981
Fifth Reprint 1985

Cover photographs
by courtesy of
Van Phillips
and J. Allan Cash Ltd.

ISBN 0 00 433970 3
© William Collins Sons & Co. Ltd. 1981
Printed in Great Britain
Collins Clear-Type Press

Contents

Contents

For this Phrase Book, we hope we've thought of *almost* everything. If you can't speak Spanish, the Collins Spanish Phrase Book can help you say what you want whenever you want.

We've thought of what you'll be doing – driving and parking the car, having a drink in a café, buying stamps for your postcards. Each page has a clear heading so you can find your place quickly, and each section contains the phrases you are genuinely likely to need.

We've put ourselves in your shoes and tried to think of the situations that could catch you out. Have you ever been faced with an exotic dish and wanted to know the right way to eat it? or how to ask for a babysitter? These are just the kind of practical questions that you'll find here. And they are in simple but idiomatic Spanish, with an easy-to-read pronunciation included.

Besides questions and phrases, we give you the information you need. Many sections begin with a few helpful tips on subjects like using the telephone or travelling by bus. There's a guide to food and wine, so you'll know what to try out, and a full set of conversion tables for everything from tyre pressures to shoe sizes. Bon voyage!

A Word of Advice

This book has been planned to make everything as easy to find as possible, but so that you won't have to fumble when you want a phrase in a hurry, try to read it through before you go away. There's no need to try and learn anything: just remember where the various sections come in the book. It will often be a good idea to look up a key word in the index, and this will take you to what you want to say.

How to Pronounce Spanish

We've tried to make the pronunciation helps under the translations as clear as possible; after all, you don't want to be looking up these pages all the time. We've broken the words up into syllables to make them easy to read, but don't pause between the syllables. The syllable to be stressed is shown in heavy type. Spanish is a fairly easy language to read, and before long you may find yourself able to read straight from the translations. Here are some points to remember.

A few sounds may give you a little trouble, for instance the letter *r,* which has to be properly rolled, not ignored as it often is in English.

The letter *c* before *e* or *i* and the letter *z* are pronounced like the *th* in *thin*.

The letter *g* before *e* or *i* and the letter *j* have the guttural sound you hear in the Scottish word *loch,* which we show here as *kh*.

The letter *h* is never pronounced.

The letters *ll* are pronounced as in million.

The letter *v* is pronounced as a *b*: *vino* is pronounced as *bee-nō*.

In English *a, i* and *o* often represent double vowel sounds (listen carefully to *late, bite, note*). In Spanish, vowels are always single sounds. When you find two together, for instance in *aceite,* you have to pronounce both of them in quick succession: *a-the-ee-tay*.

Any sounds not explained here or in the table opposite will be clear from the pronunciations.

Finally, remember that the pronunciation given here is that used in Spain itself. You'll be easily understood in South America, but what you hear will be rather different.

How to Pronounce Spanish

Spanish spelling	Closest English sound	Shown here by	Example	
a	father	*a*	padre	**pa**-*dray*
e	gate	*ay*	peseta	*pe-***say**-*ta*
	or pet	*e*	pero	**pe**-*rō*
i	feed	*ee*	litro	**lee**-*trō*
o	note	*ō*	como	**kō**-*mō*
	or (UK) pot (US) thought	*o*	dónde	**don**-*day*
u	moon	*oo*	algún	*al-***goon**
	or quick	*w*	cuando	**kwan**-*dō*
y	you	*y*	yo	*yō*
c	before a, o, u, cat	*k*	calle	**kal**-*yay*
	before e, i thin	*th*	centro	**then**-*trō*
g	before a, o, u, got	*g*	gato	**ga**-*tō*
	before e, i loch	*kh*	gente	**khen**-*tay*
j	loch	*kh*	jueves	**khway**-*bays*
ll	million	*l-y*	calle	**kal**-*yay*
ñ	onion	*n-y*	niño	**neen**-*yō*
qu	quay	*k*	queso	**kay**-*sō*
r	carrot, *rolled*	*r/rr*	ropa	**rō**-*pa*
s	sat	*s*	sábado	**sa**-*ba-dō*
v	bat	*b*	vino	**bee**-*nō*
z	thin	*th*	zumo	**thoo**-*mō*

Everyday Phrases

To start off, a few phrases you can use for basic contact with the Spaniard in the street.

Good morning – Buenos días
*bway-nōs **dee**-as*

Good afternoon
Good evening } – Buenas tardes
*bway-nas **tar**-days*

Good night – Buenas noches
*bway-nas **no**-chays*

Goodbye – Adiós
*a-**dyōs***

Yes – Sí
see

No – No
nō

O.K. – ¡Vale!
***ba**-lay!*

How are you? – ¿Cómo está usted?
*kō-mō es-**ta** oos-**ted**?*

I'm very well – Estoy muy bien
*es-**toy** mwee byen*

Please – Por favor
*por fa-**bor***

Yes please – Sí, por favor
*see, por fa-**bor***

Thank you – Gracias
***grath**-yas*

No thank you – No, gracias
*nō, **grath**-yas*

Thank you, that's very kind – Se lo agradezco mucho
of you *say lō a-grā-**deth**-kō **moo**-chō*

You're welcome – De nada
*day **na**-da*

Everyday Phrases

I'm sorry –	Lo siento
	lō syen-tō
Sorry, *or* excuse me –	Perdón
	per-don
Excuse me, please –	Oiga, por favor
	oy-ga, por fa-bor
It doesn't matter –	No importa
	no eem-por-ta
I don't mind –	No me importa
	nō may eem-por-ta
What is your name? –	¿Cómo se llama usted?
	kō-mō say lya-ma oos-ted?
My name is Mark Roberts –	Me llamo Mark Roberts
	may lya-mō Mark Roberts
I come from America –	Soy americano
	soy a-may-ree-ka-nō
I come from Britain –	Soy británico
	soy bree-ta-nee-kō
I live in Chester –	Vivo en Chester
	bee-bō en ches-ter
I am on holiday –	Estoy de vacaciones
	es-toy day ba-kath-yo-nays
See you soon –	Hasta pronto
	as-ta pron-tō

Your First Questions

You won't go very far before you want to ask questions like these. We may not have given the exact question you need, and you may have to change a few words, but you should manage. The key parts of some very common questions are in capitals; you can vary the ending yourself as circumstances require.

I WANT a single room	QUERÍA una habitación individual *kay-**ree**-a **oo**-na a-bee-tath-**yon** een-dee-beed-**wal***
WE WANT to buy some presents	QUEREMOS comprar unos regalos *kay-**ray**-mōs kom-**prar** oo-nōs ray-**ga**-lōs*
How much does that cost?	¿Cuánto cuesta eso? ***kwan**-tō **kwes**-ta e-sō?*
I WANT to make a phone call	QUIERO llamar por teléfono *kyay-rō lya-**mar** por tay-**lay**-fo-nō*
I NEED a doctor	NECESITO un médico *nay-thay-**see**-tō oon **me**-dee-kō*
WHERE IS the Tourist Information Office?	¿DÓNDE ESTÁ la oficina de Turismo? ***don**-day es-**ta** la o-fee-**thee**-na day too-**rees**-mō?*
WE ARE LOOKING FOR a camping site	BUSCAMOS un camping *boos-**ka**-mōs oon **kam**-peeng*
DO YOU KNOW a good restaurant?	¿CONOCE un buen restaurante? *ko-**no**-thay oon bwen res-tow-**ran**-tay?*
SHOULD WE reserve a table?	¿SERÁ NECESARIO reservar mesa? *say-**ra** nay-thay-**sar**-yō ray-ser-**bar** **may**-sa?*
CAN I rent a car?	¿PUEDO alquilar un coche? ***pway**-dō al-kee-**lar** oon **ko**-chay?*
How long will we have to wait?	¿Cuánto tiempo tendremos que esperar? ***kwan**-tō **tyem**-pō ten-**dray**-mōs kay es-pay-**rar**?*
What time is it please?	¿Qué hora es, por favor? *kay **o**-ra es, por fa-**bor**?*

Your First Questions

WHAT TIME do you close? – ¿A QUÉ HORA cierran?
*a kay o-ra **thye**-rran?*

WHEN IS THE NEXT TRAIN to Seville? – ¿CUANDO SALE EL PRÓXIMO TREN para Sevilla?
*kwan-dō **sa**-lay el **prok**-see-mō tren **pa**-ra say-**beel**-ya?*

CAN YOU LEND me a pen? – ¿PODRÍA PRESTARME un bolígrafo?
*po-**dree**-a pres-**tar**-may oon bo-**lee**-gra-fō?*

DO I HAVE TIME TO buy a magazine? – ¿ME DA TIEMPO A comprar una revista?
*may da **tyem**-pō a kom-**prar** oo-na ray-**bees**-ta?*

What is this? – ¿Qué es esto?
*kay es **es**-tō?*

Who did this? – ¿Quién hizo esto?
*kyen **ee**-thō **es**-tō?*

I would like to see the manager – Quería ver al director
*kay-**ree**-a ber al dee-rek-**tor***

HAVE YOU GOT any matches? – ¿TIENE cerillas?
*tyay-nay thay-**reel**-yas?*

Do you mind if I . . .? – ¿Le importa que . . .?
*lay eem-**por**-ta kay . . .?*

Problems

Of course we hope you won't have any, and that if you do they're minor ones and not real emergencies. The phrases we've given here cover both and are meant to help you through any difficulties that may come along.

Can you help me please?	– ¿Puede ayudarme por favor? *pway-day a-yoo-**dar**-may por fa-**bor**?*
Would you come with me please?	– ¿Podría usted venir conmigo, por favor? *po-**dree**-a oos-**ted** bay-**neer** kon-**mee**-go, por fa-**bor**?*
What is the matter?	– ¿Qué pasa? *kay **pa**-sa?*
What do you think is wrong?	– ¿Qué cree usted que pasa? *kay **kray**-ay oos-**ted** kay **pa**-sa?*
I don't understand	– No entiendo *nō ent-**yen**-dō*
I don't speak Spanish	– No hablo español *nō **a**-blō es-pan-**yol***
Please repeat that	– ¿Puede repetir eso, por favor? *pway-day ray-pay-teer e-sō, por fa-**bor**?*
I need someone who speaks English	– Necesito a alguien que hable inglés *nay-thay-**see**-tō a **alg**-yen kay **a**-blay eeng-**glays***
I haven't enough money	– No tengo dinero suficiente *no **teng**-gō dee-**nay**-rō soo-feeth-**yen**-tay*
I have no money	– No tengo dinero *no **teng**-gō dee-**nay**-rō*
Is there somewhere open where we can eat?	– ¿Hay algún sitio abierto para comer? *a-ee al-**goon** seet-yō ab-**yer**-tō **pa**-ra ko-**mer**?*
That man keeps following me	– Ese hombre me está siguiendo *e-say **om**-bray may es-**ta** seeg-**yen**-dō*
Stop following me	– Deje de seguirme ***day**-khay day say-**geer**-may*

Problems

Call the police –	Llame a la policía *lya-may a la po-lee-thee-a*
My car has been broken into –	Me han forzado la cerradura del coche *may an for-tha-dō la thay-rra-doo-ra del ko-chay*
My son is lost –	Mi hijo se ha perdido *mee ee-khō say a per-dee-dō*
Where is the police station? –	¿Dónde está la comisaría de policía? *don-day es-ta la ko-mee-sa-ree-a day po-lee-thee-a?*
I have lost my passport –	He perdido el pasaporte *ay per-dee-dō el pa-sa-por-tay*
My wallet has been stolen –	Me han robado la cartera *may an rō-ba-dō la kar-tay-ra*
The insurance company requires me to report it –	La compañía de seguros me exige que lo notifique *la kom-pan-yee-a day say-goo-rōs may ek-see-khay kay lō nō-tee-fee-kay*
I want to see a lawyer –	Quiero ver a un abogado *kyay-rō ber a oon a-bō-ga-dō*
Please give me my passport back –	Devuélvame el pasaporte, por favor *day-bwel-ba-may el pa-sa-por-tay, por fa-bor*
Where is the British Consulate? –	¿Dónde está el Consulado Británico? *don-day es-ta el kon-soo-la-dō bree-ta-nee-kō?*
There is a fire –	Hay un incendio *a-ee oon een-thend-yō*
There has been an accident –	Ha habido un accidente *a a-bee-dō oon ak-thee-den-tay*
Call an ambulance –	Llame a una ambulancia *lya-may a oo-na am-boo-lan-thya*
I need a doctor –	Necesito un médico *nay-thay-see-tō oon me-dee-kō*

Problems

I feel ill –	Me siento mal
	*may **syen**-tō mal*
He has hurt himself –	Se ha hecho daño
	*say a **ay**-chō **dan**-yō*
My car won't start –	No me arranca el coche
	*nō may a-**rrang**-ka el **ko**-chay*
There is something wrong with the brakes –	Los frenos no van bien
	*los **fray**-nōs nō ban byen*
The machine is broken –	El aparato está estropeado
	*el a-pa-**ra**-tō es-**ta** es-tro-pay-a-dō*
The air-conditioning does not work –	El aire acondicionado no funciona
	*el **a**-ee-ray a-kon-deeth-yo-**na**-dō nō foong-**thyo**-na*
I am in a hurry –	Tengo prisa
	***teng**-gō **pree**-sa*
I am late –	Voy retrasado
	*boy ray-tra-**sa**-dō*
How long will this take? –	¿Cuánto tardará ésto?
	***kwan**-tō tar-da-**ra** es-tō?*
How long will the delay be? –	¿Cuánto se retrasará?
	***kwan**-tō say ray-tra-sa-**ra**?*
I am leaving tomorrow. Can you do it at once? –	Me marcho mañana. ¿Puede hacerlo inmediatamente?
	*may **mar**-chō man-**ya**-na. **pway**-day a-**ther**-lō een-may-dya-ta-**men**-tay?*
I have forgotten my key –	Me he olvidado la llave
	*may ay ol-bee-**da**-dō la **lya**-bay*
I have left my bag in the toilet (restroom) –	Me he dejado el bolso en los servicios
	*may ay day-**kha**-dō el **bol**-sō en lōs ser-**beeth**-yōs*
My luggage has not arrived –	No ha llegado mi equipaje
	*nō a lyay-**ga**-dō mee ay-kee-**pa**-khay*
I have missed my train –	He perdido el tren
	*ay per-**dee**-dō el tren*

Problems

The people who were to meet me have not turned up	– Las personas que venían a recogerme no han aparecido *las per-so-nas kay bay-nee-an a ray-ko-kher-may nō an a-pa-ray-thee-dō*
My party has left without me	– Mi grupo se ha marchado sin mí *mee groo-pō say a mar-cha-dō seen mee*
I have lost my way. How do I get to the station?	– Me he perdido. ¿Cómo voy a la estación? *may ay per-dee-dō. kō-mo boy a la es-tath-yon?*
I have broken my glasses	– Se me han roto las gafas *say may an rō-tō las ga-fas*
I have spilt something	– He derramado algo *ay day-rra-ma-dō al-gō*
My clothes are soaked. Where can I dry them?	– Tengo la ropa calada. ¿Dónde puedo secarla? *teng-gō la rō-pa ka-la-da. don-day pway-dō say-kar-la?*

When You Arrive
The Formalities

Entering Spain is usually a simple business. You may possibly be stopped and asked a few questions – the answers given here should be adequate. The two customs channels are red (*Objetos a Declarar*) for dutiable goods, and green (*Nada que Declarar*) if you have nothing to declare.

Here is my passport – Aquí está mi pasaporte
a-kee es-ta mee pa-sa-por-tay

My wife and I are on a joint passport – Mi esposa y yo tenemos un pasaporte familiar
mee es-pō-sa ee yō tay-nay-mōs oon pa-sa-por-tay fa-meel-yar

Here is my driving licence and green card – Aquí está mi carnet de conducir y la carta verde
a-kee es-ta mee kar-nay day kon-doo-theer ee la kar-ta ber-day

I am staying for 2 weeks – Me voy a quedar dos semanas
may boy a kay-dar dōs say-ma-nas

We are visiting some friends – Vamos a visitar a unos amigos
ba-mōs a bee-see-tar a oo-nōs a-mee-gōs

I have nothing to declare – No tengo nada que declarar
no teng-gō na-da kay day-kla-rar

I have the usual allowances of tobacco and spirits (liquor) – Llevo la cantidad permitida de tabaco y alcohol
lyay-bō la kan-tee-dad per-mee-tee-da day ta-ba-ko ee al-kol

That is for my personal use – Eso es para mi uso personal
e-sō es pa-ra mee oo-sō per-sō-nal

How much do I have to pay? – ¿Cuánto tengo que pagar?
kwan-tō teng-gō kay pa-gar?

Where do I get the flight to Seville? – ¿De dónde sale el vuelo de Sevilla?
day don-day sa-lay el bway-lō day say-beel-ya?

Is there a bus into town? – ¿Hay algún autobús al centro de la ciudad?
a-ee al-goon ow-tō-boos al then-trō day la thyoo-dad?

When You Arrive
Your Luggage

Where is the luggage from the London flight? – ¿Dónde está el equipaje del vuelo de Londres?
*don-day es-**ta** el ay-kee-**pa**-khay del **bway**-lō day **lon**-drays?*

My suitcase is stuck on the conveyor belt – Se me ha atascado la maleta en la cinta transportadora
*say may a a-tas-**ka**-dō la ma-**lay**-ta en la **theen**-ta trans-por-ta-**do**-ra*

Are there any porters? – ¿Hay maleteros?
*a-ee ma-lay-**tay**-rōs?*

Are there any luggage trolleys (carriers)? – ¿Hay carritos para transportar el equipaje?
*a-ee ka-**rree**-tōs **pa**-ra trans-por-**tar** el ay-kee-**pa**-khay?*

Is there any charge? – ¿Hay que abonar algo?
*a-ee kay a-bo-**nar** al-gō?*

Is there a left-luggage office (baggage room)? – ¿Hay Consigna?
*a-ee kon-**seeg**-na?*

Please take these bags to a taxi – Lleve estas maletas a un taxi, por favor
*lyay-bay es-tas ma-**lay**-tas a oon **tak**-see por fa-**bor***

I'll carry that myself – Eso lo llevo yo
*e-sō lō **lyay**-bō yō*

Careful, the handle is broken – Cuidado, el asa está rota
*kwee-**da**-dō, el **a**-sa es-**ta** rō-ta*

No, don't put that on top! – ¡No, no ponga eso encima!
*nō, nō **pong**-ga e-sō en-**thee**-ma!*

That case is not mine – Esa maleta no es mía
*e-sa ma-**lay**-ta nō es **mee**-a*

Where is my other case? – ¿Dónde está mi otra maleta?
*don-day es-**ta** mee ō-tra ma-**lay**-ta?*

Asking the way
Things you'll hear

It's no good being able to ask the way if you're not going to understand the directions you get. We've tried to anticipate the likely answers, so listen carefully for these key phrases.

Vaya – **recto**
ba-ya *rek*-tō
You go straight on

– **a la derecha**
*a la day-**ray**-cha*
right

– **a la izquierda**
*a la eeth-**kyer**-da*
left

– **hasta**
as-ta
as far as

Tuerza *or* **gire** – **a la derecha**
twer-tha or ***khee**-ray* *a la day-**ray**-cha*
Turn right

– **a la izquierda**
*a la eeth-**kyer**-da*
left

Siga – **hasta**
see-ga *as-ta*
Keep going straight ahead as far as

Coja – **la primera (calle) a la derecha**
ko-kha *la pree-**may**-ra (**kal**-yay) a la day-**ray**-cha*
Take the first (street) on the right

– **la segunda (carretera) a la izquierda**
*la say-**goon**-da (ka-rray-**tay**-ra) a la
eeth-**kyer**-da*
the second (road) on the left

Siga las señales *or* – Follow the signs for
indicaciones de
see-ga las sayn-**ya**-lays or
*een-dee-kath-**yo**-nays day*

Asking the way
Things you'll hear

Cruce – **la calle**
kroo-thay   *la kal-yay*
Cross   the street

– **la plaza**
la pla-tha
the square

– **el paso a nivel**
el pa-sō a nee-bel
at the level crossing

Está – **en el cruce**
es-ta   *en el kroo-thay*
It's   at the junction (intersection)

– **junto al teatro**
khoon-tō al tay-a-trō
next to the theatre

– **después del semáforo**
des-pways del say-ma-fo-rō
after the traffic lights

– **frente a la iglesia**
fren-tay a la ee-glay-sya
opposite the church

– **al dar la vuelta a la esquina**
al dar la bwel-ta a la es-kee-na
around the corner

– **en el próximo piso**
en el prok-see-mō pee-sō
on the next floor

– **allí**
al-yee
over there

If you're completely on the wrong track, you may be told:

Tiene que dar la vuelta – You have to turn around
tyay-nay kay dar la bwel-ta

Asking the Way

Excuse me, please . . . –	Oiga, por favor . . . *oy-ga, por fa-bor . . .*
Where is the cathedral? –	¿Dónde está la catedral? *don-day es-ta la ka-tay-dral?*
Can you tell me the way to the airport? –	¿Puede decirme por dónde se va al aeropuerto? *pway-day day-theer-may por don-day say ba al a-ay-rō-pwer-tō?*
Is there a service station near here? –	¿Hay una estación de servicio cerca de acquí? *a-ee oo-na es-ta-thyon day ser-beeth-yō ther-ka day a-kee?*
Where are the toilets? –	¿Dónde están los servicios? *don-day es-tan los ser-beeth-yōs?*
Where is the nearest post office? –	¿Dónde hay una oficina de correos? *don-day a-ee oo-na o-fee-thee-na day co-rray-ōs?*
Is this the right way to the castle? –	¿Voy bien por aquí para el castillo? *boy byen por a-kee pa-ra el kas-teel-yō?*
How long will it take to get there? –	¿Cuánto se tarda en llegar? *kwan-tō say tar-da en lyay-gar?*
Is it far? –	¿Está lejos? *es-ta lay-khōs?*
Can you walk there? –	¿Se puede ir caminando? *say pway-day eer ka-mee-nan-dō?*
Is there a bus that goes there? –	¿Hay autobús hasta allá? *a-ee ow-tō-boos as-ta al-ya?*
Where do I get the bus for Oviedo? –	¿Dónde cojo el autobús para Oviedo? *don-day ko-khō el ow-tō-boos pa-ra ob-yay-dō?*
Is there a youth hostel near here? –	¿Hay un albergue juvenil cerca de aquí? *a-ee oon al-ber-gay khoo-bay-neel ther-ka day a-kee?*
I have lost my way	Me he perdido *may ay per-dee-dō*

Asking the Way

I am trying to get to the centre of the city	– Quiero ir al centro de la ciudad *kyay-rō eer al **then**-trō day la thyoo-**dad***
I am looking for the Tourist Information Office	– Estoy buscando la oficina de Información y Turismo *es-**toy** boos-**kan**-dō la o-fee-**thee**-na de een-for-math-**yon** ee too-**rees**-mō*
Can you show me on the map?	– ¿Puede indicármelo en el mapa? *pway-day een-dee-**kar**-may-lō en el **ma**-pa?*
Which road do I take for Oviedo?	– ¿Cuál es la carretera de Oviedo? *kwal es la ka-rray-**tay**-ra day ob-**yay**-dō?*
How far is it to León?	– ¿A qué distancia está León? *a kay dees-**tan**-thya es-**ta** lay-**on**?*
Will we arrive by this evening?	– ¿Estaremos allí esta noche? *es-ta-**ray**-mōs al-**yee** es-ta **no**-chay?*
Which is the best route to Valencia?	– ¿Cual es el mejor itinerario para ir a Valencia? *kwal es el may-**khor** ee-tee-nay-**ra**-ryō **pa**-ra eer a ba-**lenth**-ya?*
Which is the most scenic route?	– ¿Cual es la ruta más pintoresca? *kwal es la **roo**-ta mas peen-tō-**res**-ka?*
Do I turn here for Valencia?	– ¿Tuerzo aquí para ir a Valencia? ***twer**-thō a-**kee pa**-ra ba-**len**-thya?*
Is the traffic one-way?	– ¿Es una zona de direcciones únicas? *es **oo**-na **thō**-na day dee-rek-**thyo**-nays **oo**-nee-kas?*
How do I get onto the motorway (highway)?	– ¿Por dónde voy para la autopista? *por **don**-day boy **pa**-ra la ow-tō-**pees**-ta?*
Where does this road go to?	– ¿A dónde va esta carretera? *a **don**-day ba **es**-ta ka-rray-**tay**-ra?*

Buses & Metro

On buses you can pay as you enter, or buy a *bonobús* for ten bus-rides over any distance. A single ticket on the metro in Madrid and Barcelona will take you as far as you want to go, and 7-day tickets allow you unlimited travel for a week.

Which bus do I take for the Prado? – ¿Qué autobús cojo para ir al Prado?
*kay ow-tō-**boos** ko-khō **pa**-ra eer al **pra**-dō?*

Where do I get a bus for Bilbao? – ¿Dónde cojo un autobús para Bilbao?
***don**-day ko-khō oon ow-tō-**boos** **pa**-ra beel-**ba**-ō?*

Does this bus go to the Liceo? – ¿Este autobús va al Liceo?
***es**-te ow-tō-**boos** ba al lee-**thay**-ō?*

Where should I change? – ¿Dónde tengo que cambiar?
***don**-day **teng**-gō kay kam-**byar**?*

I want to go to the Puerta del Sol – Quiero ir a la Puerta del Sol
***kyay**-rō eer a la **pwer**-ta del sol*

How much is the fare please? – ¿Cuanto es, por favor?
***kwan**-tō es por fa-**bor**?*

A 7-day ticket please – Un abono para siete días, por favor
*oon a-**bo**-nō **pa**-ra **syay**-tay **dee**-as, por fa-**bor***

Will you let me off at the right stop? – ¿Me puede avisar cuando llegue a la parada, por favor?
*may **pway**-day a-bee-**sar** **kwan**-dō **lyay**-gay a la pa-**ra**-da, por fa-**bor**?*

When is the last bus? – ¿A qué hora es el último autobús?
*a kay ō-ra es el **ool**-tee-mō ow-tō-**boos**?*

How long does it take to get to La Zarzuela? – ¿Cuánto se tarda en llegar a La Zarzuela?
***kwan**-tō say **tar**-da en lyay-**gar** a la thar-**thway**-la?*

How frequent is the service? – ¿Con qué frecuencia pasan los autobuses?
*kon kay fray-**kwen**-thya **pa**-san lōs ow-tō-**boo**-ses?*

You can hail a taxi or pick it up at a stand; the driver will expect a tip of about ten per cent.

Chamartin Station, please – A la estación de Chamartín, por favor
*a la es-tath-**yon** day cha-mar-**teen**, por fa-**bor***

30, Calle de Serrano, please – Calle de Serrano, número treinta, por favor
kal**-yay day se-**rra**-nō, **noo**-may-rō **tre**-een-ta, por fa-**bor

Please take me to this address – Lléveme a esta dirección, por favor
lyay**-bay-may a **es**-ta dee-rek-**thyon**, por fa-**bor

Will you put the luggage in the boot (trunk)? – ¿Puede meter el equipaje en el maletero?
***pway**-day me-**ter** el ay-kee-**pa**-khay en el ma-lay-**tay**-rō?*

Please drive us round the town – Dénos una vuelta por la ciudad, por favor
day**-nōs **oo**-na **bwel**-ta por la **thyoo**-dad, por fa-**bor

I'm in a hurry – Tengo prisa
***teng**-gō **pree**-sa*

Please wait here for a few minutes – Espere aquí un momento, por favor
*es-**pay**-ray a-**kee** oon mō-**men**-tō, por fa-**bor***

Turn left please – Tuerza a la izquierda, por favor
twer**-tha a la eeth-**kyer**-da, por fa-**bor

Turn right please – Tuerza a la derecha, por favor
twer**-tha a la day-**ray**-cha, por fa-**bor

Please stop at the corner – Pare ahí en la esquina, por favor
pa**-ray a-**ee** en la es-**kee**-na, por fa-**bor

How much is that please? – ¿Cuánto es, por favor?
***kwan**-tō es, por fa-**bor**?*

Keep the change – Quédese con el cambio
***kay**-day-say kon el **kam**-byō*

Trains
Your Ticket

If you are travelling on one of the busy main routes, it is a good idea to reserve your seat in advance. A supplement is payable on some of the luxury trains like the *TALGO* or the *TER*. Within Spain children between 3 and 7 pay half-fare, and younger ones travel free. *Billetes kilométricos* are available for those who want to go a long way – a book of coupons entitles you to a discount on your fare over distances of 3,000 km or more. Smoking is not allowed in the compartments of Spanish trains – if you want a cigarette you will have to stand in the corridor.

For night journeys you can reserve either a sleeper or a couchette, which is a simple berth in a compartment shared by several passengers.

A single (one-way ticket) to Madrid, please – Un billete para Madrid, por favor
*oon beel-**yay**-tay **pa**-ra ma-**dreed**, por fa-bor*

A return (round-trip ticket) to Madrid, please – Un billete de ida y vuelta para Madrid, por favor
*oon beel-**yay**-tay day ee-da ee **bwel**-ta **pa**-ra ma-**dreed**, por fa-**bor***

A child's return to Madrid, please – Un billete de niño para Madrid, ida y vuelta, por favor
*oon beel-**yay**-tay day **neen**-yō **pa**-ra ma-**dreed**, ee-da ee **bwel**-ta, por fa-**bor***

A return to Madrid, first class – Un billete de primera para Madrid, ida y vuelta, por favor
*oon beel-**yay**-tay day pree-**may**-ra **pa**-ra ma-**dreed**, ee-da ee **bwel**-ta, por fa-**bor***

I want to book a seat on the 1030 train to Santander – Quiero reservar un asiento en el tren de las diez treinta a Santander
kyay**-rō ray-ser-**bar** oon a-**syen**-tō en el tren day las dyeth **tre**-een-ta a san-tan-**der

Second class, by the window, please – Segunda, junto a la ventana, por favor
*say-**goon**-da, **khoon**-tō a la ben-**ta**-na por fa-**bor***

Trains
Your Luggage

Can I have a sleeper on the night train to La Coruña? –
Un coche-cama en el tren de la noche a La Coruña, por favor
*oon **ko**-chay **ka**-ma en el tren day la **no**-chay a la ko-**roon**-ya, por fa-**bor***

Can I have a couchette on the 2200 to La Coruña? –
Una litera en el tren de las veintidós horas a la Coruña, por favor
*oo-na lee-**tay**-ra en el tren day las be-een-tee-**dos** ō-ras a la ko-**roon**-ya, por fa-**bor***

Can I register (check) my luggage? –
¿Puedo facturar el equipaje?
*pway-dō fak-too-**rar** el ay-kee-**pa**-khay?*

I want to register these cases –
Quiero facturar estas maletas
*kyay-rō fak-too-**rar** es-tas ma-**lay**-tas*

Where do I pick up my registered luggage? –
¿Dónde se recoge el equipaje facturado?
*don-day say ray-**ko**-khay el ay-kee-**pa**-khay fak-too-**ra**-dō?*

I want to leave these bags in the left luggage (baggage room) –
Quiero dejar estas maletas en Consigna
*kyay-rō day-**khar** es-tas ma-**lay**-tas en kon-**seeg**-na*

I shall pick them up this evening –
Las recogeré esta tarde
*las ray-ko-khay-**ray** es-ta **tar**-day*

What time do you close? –
¿A qué hora cierran?
*a kay ō-ra **thye**-rran?*

How much is it per suitcase? –
¿Cuanto es cada maleta?
*kwan-tō es **ka**-da ma-**lay**-ta?*

Please take these bags to platform 9 –
Lleve estas maletas al andén número nueve, por favor
*lyay-bay es-tas ma-**lay**-tas al an-**den** noo-may-rō **nway**-bay, por fa-**bor***

Would you look after these bags for a minute please? –
¿Podría cuidarme estas maletas un momento, por favor?
*po-**dree**-a kwee-**dar**-may es-tas ma-**lay**-tas oon mō-**men**-tō, por fa-**bor**?*

Trains
Boarding the Train

Where is the departure board (listing)?	– ¿Dónde está el horario de salidas? *don-day es-ta el ō-rar-yō day sa-lee-das?*
When is the next train to Bilbao?	– ¿A qué hora sale el próximo tren para Bilbao? *a kay ō-ra sa-lay el prok-see-mō tren pa-ra beel-ba-ō?*
What are the times of trains to Bilbao?	– ¿Cual es el horario de trenes a Bilbao? *kwal es el ō-rar-yō day tray-nays a beel-ba-ō?*
What time is the last train to Bilbao?	– ¿A qué hora sale el último tren para Bilbao? *a kay ō-ra sa-lay el ool-tee-mō tren pa-ra beel-ba-ō?*
What platform do I go to for the Madrid train?	– ¿De qué andén sale el tren de Madrid? *day kay an-den sa-lay el tren day ma-dreed?*
Is this the right platform for Madrid?	– ¿Es este el andén para Madrid? *es es-tay el an-den pa-ra ma-dreed?*
Is this the Madrid train?	– ¿Es este el tren para Madrid? *es es-tay el tren pa-ra ma-dreed?*
What time does the train leave?	– ¿A qué hora sale el tren? *a kay ō-ra sa-lay el tren?*
Is there a dining car?	– ¿Lleva vagón-restaurante este tren? *lyay-ba ba-gon res-tow-ran-tay es-tay tren?*
Is there a buffet (club) car?	– ¿Lleva cafetería este tren? *lyay-ba ka-fay-tay-ree-a a es-tay tren?*
What time do we get to Barcelona?	– ¿A qué hora llegamos a Barcelona? *a kay ō-ra lyay-ga-mōs a bar-thay-lō-na?*
Is this a through train?	– ¿Este tren es directo? *es-tay tren es dee-rek-tō?*
Where do I have to change for Jaca?	– ¿Dónde tengo que hacer transbordo para Jaca? *don-day teng-gō kay a-ther trans-bor-dō pa-ra kha-ka?*

Trains
In the Train

How long do I have before my next train leaves?	— ¿Cuanto me falta para hacer transbordo? *kwan-tō may **fal**-ta **pa**-ra a-**ther** trans-**bor**-dō?*
Is this seat taken?	— ¿Está ocupado este asiento? *es-**ta** o-koo-**pa** dō os tay a **syen**-tō.'*
This is my seat	— Este es mi asiento *es-tay es mee a-**syen**-tō*
Can you help me with my bags please?	— ¿Puede ayudarme con estas maletas, por favor? *pway-day a-yoo-**dar**-may kon es-tas ma-**lay**-tas, por fa-**bor**?*
May I open the window?	— ¿Puedo abrir la ventana? *pway-**dō** a-breer la ben-**ta**-na?*
This is a no-smoking compartment	— Está prohibido fumar aquí *es-**ta** pro-ee-**bee**-dō foo-**mar** a-kee*
My wife has my ticket	— Mi esposa tiene mi billete *me es-**pō**-sa **tyay**-nay mee beel-**yay**-tay*
Do we stop at Zaragoza?	— ¿Paramos en Zaragoza? *pa-**ra**-mōs en tha-ra-**go**-tha?*
Are we at Zaragoza yet?	— ¿Hemos llegado ya a Zaragoza? ***ay**-mōs lyay-**ga**-dō ya a tha-ra-**go**-tha?*
Are we running late?	— ¿Llevamos algún retraso? *lyay-**ba**-mōs al-**goon** ray-**tra**-sō?*

Driving
Service Station

LA GASOLINA – petrol or gas – comes in two varieties in Spain – *normal* (=2 star) and *super* (=4 star). We've set out conversion tables on pages 116 and 117 for you to work out how many litres to ask for, and to tell you what your metric tyre-pressure should be.

15 litres of Quince litros de ***keen**-thay **lee**-trōs day*	– **2 star** normal *nor-**mal***
	– **4 star** super ***soo**-per*
	– **diesel fuel** gas-oil *gas-o-**eel***
1,000 pesetas worth please	– Mil pesetas, por favor *meel pay-**say**-tas, por fa-**bor***
Fill her up please	– Lleno, por favor *lyay-**nō**, por fa-**bor***
Check Revíseme *ray-**bee**-say-may*	– **the oil** el aceite *el a-**the**-ee-tay*
	– **the water** el agua *el **a**-gwa*
I need some distilled water	– Necesito agua destilada *nay-thay-**see**-tō **a**-gwa des-tee-**la**-da*
Check the tyre pressure please	– Revíseme la presión de los neumáticos, por favor *ra-**bee**-say-may la pre-**syon** day lōs ne-oo-**ma**-tee-kōs, por fa-**bor***
The pressure should be 2.3	– La presión tiene que ser de 2, 3 *la pre-**syon** tyay-nay kay ser day dōs **ko**-ma tres*
Could you put some water in the windscreen washer?	– ¿Puede ponerme agua en el depósito del limpiacristales? ***pway**-day po-**ner**-may **a**-gwa en el day-**po**-see-tō del leem-pya-krees-**ta**-lays*

Driving
Parking

Many Spanish towns have adopted the system of the disc zone, or *zona azul*. Here you just leave a parking disc by your windscreen, and this shows when you arrived and when you should leave. You are usually allowed to park for about one and a half hours. Away from the centre, you will find streets where parking is only allowed on one side on a given day, for example during the first half of the month or on odd-numbered dates.

Can I park here?	– ¿Puedo aparcar aquí? *pway-dō a-par-kar a-kee?*
Where is there a car park (parking lot)?	– ¿Dónde hay un aparcamiento? *don-day a-ee oon a-par-kam-yen-tō?*
Do I need a parking disc?	– ¿Hace falta disco de estacionamiento limitado? *a-thay fal-ta dees-kō day es-tath-yo-nam-yen-tō lee-mee-ta-dō?*
Where can I get a parking disc?	– ¿Dónde puedo comprar un disco de estacionamiento limitado? *don-day pway-dō kom-prar oon dees-kō day es-tath-yo-nam-yen-tō lee-mee-ta-do?*
Do I need parking lights?	– ¿Hacen falta luces de aparcamiento? *a-then fal-ta loo-thays day a-par-kam-yen-tō?*
What time does the car park close?	– ¿A qué hora cierra este aparcamiento? *a kay ō-ra thye-rra es-tay a-par-kam-yen-tō?*
How long can I stay here?	– ¿Cuanto tiempo puedo estacionar aquí? *kwan-tō tyem-pō pway-dō es-tath-yo-nar a-kee?*
Can I park on this side today?	– ¿Puedo aparcar a este lado hoy? *pway-dō a-par-kar a es-tay la-dō oy?*

Driving
Road Conditions

Are the roads to Alicante clear?	– ¿Están despejadas las carreteras a Alicante? *es-**tan** des-pay-**kha**-das las ka-rray-**tay**-ras a a-lee-**kan**-tay?*
Are there any hold-ups (tie-ups)?	– ¿Hay algún atasco? *a-ee al-**goon** a-tas-kō?*
What's causing this hold-up?	– ¿Qué está produciendo este atasco? *kay es-**ta** pro-dooth-**yen**-dō es-tay a-**tas**-kō?*
When will the road be clear?	– ¿Cuando estará la carretera despejada? ***kwan**-dō es-ta-**ra** la ka-rray-**tay**-ra des-pay-**kha**-da?*
Is there a detour?	– ¿Hay un desviamiento? *a-ee oon des-bya-**myen**-tō?*
What is the speed limit?	– ¿Qué límite de velocidad hay? *kay **lee**-mee-tay day bay-lo-thee-**dad** a-ee?*
Is the pass open?	– ¿Está abierto el puerto? *es-**ta** ab-**yer**-tō el **pwer**-tō?*
Is the tunnel open?	– ¿Está abierto el túnel? *es-**ta** ab-**yer**-tō el **too**-nel?*
How much is the toll?	– ¿Cuánto cuesta el peaje? ***kwan**-tō **kwes**-ta el pay-**a**-khay?*

Driving
Renting a Car

I want to rent a car – Quiero alquilar un coche
kyay-rō al-kee-*lar* oon *ko*-chay

I want it for 5 days – Lo quiero para cinco días
lo *kyay*-rō *pa*-ra *theen*-kō dee-as

Is there a charge for mileage? – ¿Se paga por kilometraje?
say *pa*-gu por kee-lo-may-*tra*-khay?

Do you have – **a larger car?**
¿Tienen   un coche mayor?
tyay-nen   oon *ko*-chay ma-*yor?*

– **a cheaper car?**
un coche más barato?
oon *ko*-chay mas ba-*ra*-tō?

– **an automatic?**
un automático?
oon ow-tō-*ma*-tee-kō?

My wife will be driving as – Mi mujer va a conducir también
well mee moo-*kher* ba a kon-doo-*theer*
tam-*byen*

Must I return the car here? – ¿Tengo que devolver el coche aquí?
teng-gō kay day-bol-*ber* el *ko*-chay a-*kee?*

I would like to leave the car – Quería dejar el coche en Sevilla
in Seville kay-*ree*-a day-*khar* el *ko*-chay en
say-*beel*-ya

Please show me how – **the lights work**
¿Puede enseñarme cómo   funcionan las luces?
pway-day en-se-*nyar*-may kō-mō   foong-*thyo*-nan las *loo*-thays?

– **the windscreen wipers work**
funciona el limpiaparabrisas?
foong-*thyo*-na el leem-pya-pa-ra-*bree*-sas?

Where is reverse? – ¿Dónde está la marcha atrás?
don-*day* es-*ta* la *mar*-cha a-*tras?*

Please explain the car – ¿Puede explicarme los documentos del
documents coche?
pway-day eks-plee-*kar*-may lōs
do-koo-*men*-tōs del *ko*-chay?

Driving
Breakdowns & Repairs

You should take a red warning triangle with you in case of any breakdowns or accidents.

I have had a breakdown	– He tenido una avería *ay te-nee-dō* **oo**-*na a-bay-***ree***-a*
Can you send ¿Puede mandarme ***pway****-day man-***dar***-may*	– **a mechanic?** un mecánico? *oon may-***ka***-nee-kō?*
	– **a breakdown van (tow-truck)?** una grúa? *oo-na* **groo**-*a?*
Can you take me to the **nearest garage?**	– ¿Puede llevarme al garaje mas próximo? ***pway****-day lyay-***bar***-may al ga-***ra***-khay mas* ***prok***-*see-mō?*
Can you give me a tow?	– ¿Puede remolcarme? ***pway****-day ray-mol-***kar***-may?*
I have run out of petrol (gas)	– Me he quedado sin gasolina *may ay kay-***da***-dō seen ga-sō-***lee***-na*
Can you give me a can of **petrol, please?**	– ¿Puede darme una lata de gasolina, por favor? ***pway****-day* **dar**-*may oo-na* **la**-*ta day* *ga-sō-***lee***-na, por fa-***bor***?*
There is something wrong **with my car**	– Mi coche no va bien *mee* **ko**-*chay nō ba byen*
Can you find the trouble?	– ¿Encuentra la avería? *en-***kwen***-tra la a-bay-***ree***-a?*
I have a flat tyre	– Tengo una rueda pinchada ***teng****-gō oo-na* **rway**-*da peen-***cha***-da*
The battery is dead	– La batería está descargada *la ba-tay-***ree***-a es-***ta*** *des-kar-***ga***-da*
My windscreen (windshield) **has shattered**	– El parabrisas estalló en pedazos *el pa-ra-***bree***-sas es-tal-***yō*** *en pay-***da***-thōs*
The engine is overheating	– El motor se calienta *el mō-***tor*** *say kal-***yen***-ta*

Driving
Breakdowns & Repairs

There is a leak in the radiator	El radiador pierde agua *el rad-ya-**dor** **pyer**-day **a**-gwa*
I have blown a fuse	Se ha fundido un fusible *say a foon-**dee**-dō oon foo-**see**-blay*
The exhaust-pipe has fallen off	He perdido el tubo de escape *ay per-**dee**-dō el **too**-bō day es-**ka**-pay*
There is a bad connection	Hay un cable que hace mal contacto ***a**-ee oon **ka**-blay kay **a**-thay mal kon-**tak**-tō*
I have lost the ignition key	He perdido la llave del contacto *ay per-**dee**-dō la **lya**-bay del kon-**tak**-tō*
I need a new fan belt	Necesito una correa de ventilador *nay-thay-**see**-tō **oo**-na ko-**rray**-a day ben-tee-la-**dor***
Can you replace the windscreen wiper?	¿Puede ponerme un limpiaparabrisas nuevo? ***pway**-day po-**ner**-may oon leem-pya-pa-ra-**bree**-sas **nway**-bō?*
Is it serious?	¿Es muy seria la avería? *es mwee **se**-rya la a-bay-**ree**-a?*
How long will it take to repair it?	¿Cuánto tardará en repararlo? ***kwan**-tō tar-da-**ra** en ray-pa-**rar**-lō?*
Do you have the parts?	¿Tiene los repuestos necesarios? ***tyay**-nay lōs ray-**pwes**-tōs nay-thay-**sa**-ryōs?*
Can you fix it for the time being?	¿Puede arreglarlo provisionalmente? ***pway**-day a-rray-**glar**-lō pro-bees-yo-nal-**men**-tay?*
Can I have an itemized bill for my insurance company?	¿Me da una factura completa para la compañia de seguros? *may da **oo**-na fak-**too**-ra kom-**play**-ta **pa**-ra la kom-pan-**yee**-a day say-**goo**-rōs?*

Driving The Car

accelerator	acelerador	**disc brake**	freno de disco
	a-thay-lay-ra-dor		*fray-nō day dees-kō*
air filter	filtro de aire	**distributor**	distribuidor
	feel-trō day a-ee-ray		*dees-tree-bwee-dor*
alternator	alternador	**door**	puerta
	al-ter-na-dor		*pwer-ta*
automatic	transmisión	**dynamo**	dínamo
transmis-	automática		*dee-na-mō*
sion	*trans-mees-yon*	**electrical**	sistema eléctrico
	ow-tō-ma-tee-ka	**system**	*sees-tay-ma*
axle	eje		*ay-lek-tree-kō*
	e-khay	**engine**	motor
backup light	luz de marcha		*mo-tor*
	atrás	**exhaust**	escape
	looth day mar-cha	**system**	*es-ka-pay*
	a-tras	**fan belt**	correa de
battery	batería		ventilador
	ba-te-ree-a		*ko-rray-a day*
bonnet	capó		*ben-tee-la-dor*
	ka-pō	**fuel gauge**	indicador del nivel
boot	maletero		*een-dee-ka-dor del*
	mal-lay-tay-rō		*nee-bel*
brakes	frenos	**fuel pump**	bomba de la
	fray-nōs		gasolina
brake fluid	líquido de frenos		*bom-ba day la*
	lee-kee-dō day		*ga-so-lee-na*
	fray-nōs	**fuse**	fusible
bumper	defensa		*foo-see-blay*
	day-fen-sa	**gear box**	caja de cambios
carburettor	carburador		*ka-kha day kam-byōs*
	kar-boo-ra-dor	**gear lever**	palanca de
choke	aire	**(shift)**	cambios
	a-ee-ray		*pa-lang-ka day*
clutch	embrague		*kam-byōs*
	em-bra-gay	**generator**	dínamo
cooling	sistema de		*dee-na-mō*
system	refrigeración	**handbrake**	freno de mano
	sees-tay-ma day		*fray-nō day ma-nō*
	ray-free-khay-rath-	**headlights**	faros
	yon		*fa-rōs*
cylinder	cilindro	**heating**	calefacción
	thee-leen-drō	**system**	*ka-lay-fak-thyon*

Driving
The Car

horn	claxon *klak-son*	**shock absorber**	amortiguador *a-mor-tee-gwa-dor*
hood	capó *ka-pō*	**silencer**	silenciador *see-lenth-ya-dor*
hose	manguito *mang-gee-tō*	**spanner**	llave inglesa *lya-bay een glay-sa*
ignition	encendido *en-then-dee-dō*	**spare part**	respuesto *ray-pwes-tō*
indicator	intermitente *een-ter-mee-ten-tay*	**spark plug**	bujía *boo-khee-a*
jack	gato *ga-tō*	**speedometer**	velocímetro *bay-lo-thee-may-trō*
lights	luces *loo-thays*	**starter motor**	motor de arranque *mo-tor day a-rrang-kay*
muffler	silenciador *see-lenth-ya-dor*	**steering**	dirección *dee-rekth-yon*
oil	aceite *a-the-ee-tay*	**stoplight**	chivato *chee-ba-tō*
oil filter	filtro de aceite *feel-trō day a-the-ee-tay*	**suspension**	suspensión *soos-pen-syon*
oil pressure gauge	manómetro de aceite *ma-no-may-trō day a-the-ee-tay*	**transmission**	transmisión *trans-mees-yon*
		trunk	maletero *ma-lay-tay-rō*
petrol	gasolina *ga-sō-lee-na*	**turn indicator**	intermitente *een-ter-mee-ten-tay*
radiator	radiator *rad-ya-dor*	**tyre**	cubierta *koob-yer-ta*
rear-view mirror	espejo retrovisor *es-pay-khō ray-trō bee-sor*	**warning light**	chivato *chee-ba-tō*
reversing light	luz de marcha atrás *looth day mar-cha a-tras*	**water**	agua *a-gwa*
		wheel	rueda *rway-da*
seat	asiento *as-syen-tō*	**windscreen/ windshield**	parabrisas *pa-ra-bree-sas*
seat belt	cinturón de seguridad *theen-too-ron day say-goo-ree-dad*	**wipers**	limpiaparabrisas *leem-pya-pa-ra-bree- sas*
		wrench	llave inglesa *lya-bay een-glay-sa*

Motoring
Police & Accidents

I'm very sorry officer –	Lo siento mucho, agente *lō **syen**-tō **moo**-chō a-**khen**-tay*
I did not see the signal	No ví la señal *nō bee la sayn-**yal***
I did not know about that regulation –	No conocía esa norma *nō ko-nō-**thee**-a e-sa **nor**-ma*
I did not understand the sign –	No entendí el letrero *nō en-ten-**dee** el lay-**tray**-rō*
Here is my driving licence –	Aquí está mi permiso de conducir *a-**kee** es-ta mee per-**mee**-sō day kon-doo-**theer***
Here is my green card –	Aquí está mi carta verde *a-**kee** es-**ta** mee **kar**-ta **ber**-day*
How much is the fine? –	¿Cuánto es la multa? ***kwan**-tō es la **mool**-ta?*
I haven't got that much. Can I pay at the police station? –	No tengo suficiente. ¿Puedo pagar en la comisaría de policía? *nō **teng**-gō soo-feeth-yen-tay. **pway**-dō pa-**gar** en la ko-mee-sa-**ree**-a day po-lee-**thee**-a?*
I was driving at 80 kmh –	Iba a ochenta kilómetros por hora *ee-ba a o-**chen**-ta kee-lo-may-trōs por ō-ra*
He was too close –	El estaba demasiado cerca *el es-**ta**-ba day-mas-**ya**-dō **ther**-ka*
I did not see him –	No le ví *nō lay bee*
He was driving too fast –	El iba demasiado rápido *el **ee**-ba day-mas-**ya**-dō **ra**-pee-dō*
He did not stop –	El no paró *el nō pa-**rō***
He did not give way (yield) –	No cedió el paso *no thay-**dyō** el **pa**-sō*
He stopped very suddenly –	Se paró de repente *say pa-**rō** day ray-**pen**-tay*

Motoring
Police & Accidents

He swerved –	Dió un volantazo
	dyō oon bo-lan-__ta__-thō
The car turned without –	El coche giró sin indicación
signalling	*el __ko__-chay khee-__rō__ seen een-dee-kath-__yon__*
He ran into me –	Se me echó encima
	say may ay-__chō__ en-thee-ma
He overtook on a bend –	Adelantó en una curva
(passed on a curve)	*a-day-lan-__tō__ en oo-na __koor__-ba*
His car (license) number –	Su matrícula era . . .
was . . .	*soo ma-__tree__-koo-la e-ra*
The road was wet –	La carretera estaba mojada
	la ka-rray-__tay__-ra es-ta-ba mo-__kha__-da
I skidded –	Patiné
	pa-tee-__nay__
My brakes failed –	Me fallaron los frenos
	may fa-__lya__-ron lōs __fray__-nōs
I had a blow-out –	Me reventó una rueda
	may ray-ben-__tō__ oo-na __rway__-da
I could not stop in time –	No pude parar a tiempo
	nō __poo__-day pa-__rar__ a __tyem__-pō
What is your name and –	¿Su nombre y dirección por favor?
address?	*soo __nom__-bray ee dee-rekth-__yon__ por fa-__bor__?*
We should call the police –	Deberíamos llamar a la policía
	day-bay-__ree__-a-mōs lya-__mar__ a la
	po-lee-__thee__-a

Hotels

Hotels are grouped into categories of from one to five stars, and boarding houses (*pensiones* and *hostales*) are graded one, two or three stars. Two other types of accommodation are worth noting: the *paradores nacionales*, often converted historical buildings in beautiful settings, and the *albergues de carretera*, set at strategic points on main roads and motorways.

Many hotels can handle a reservation in English, but if you don't want to take any chances . . .

Dear Sirs,
  Estimados señores:
    I wish to stay in Granada from 5/6/85 to 9/6/85
  Deseo permanecer en Granada desde el día 5-6-85 hasta el 9-6-85
    – **with my wife**
      con mi esposa
    – **with my family**
      con mi familia
Can you provide the following accommodation
  Desearía me reservasen el siguiente alojamiento
    – **1 single room with shower**
      una habitación individual con ducha
    – **1 room with twin beds and bath**
      una habitación de dos camas con baño
    – **1 room with a double bed**
      una habitación doble
    – **1 double room with a bed for a child**
      una habitación doble con una cama para un niño
and inform me of your inclusive rates for
  y me informasen de sus tarifas (servicios e impuestos incluidos) por
    – **room and breakfast**
      habitación y desayuno
    – **room and evening meal**
      media pensión
    – **room and all meals**
      pensión completa
Yours faithfully,
  Atentamente,

Hotels

You'll have to cope with the reply yourself, but if everything is all right it will mention prices; if it begins '*sentimos mucho*' or '*lamentamos comunicarle*' you may have problems.

My name is . . .	Soy . . . *soy*
I reserved a room	Tengo reservada una habitación ***teng**-gō ray-ser-**ba**-da **oo**-na a-bee-tath-**yon***
Do you have a single room?	¿Tiene una habitación individual? ***tyay**-nay **oo**-na a-bee-tath-**yon** een-dee-bee-**dwal**?*
Do you have a room with twin beds and shower?	¿Tiene una habitación de dos camas con ducha? ***tyay**-nay **oo**-na a-bee-tath-**yon** day dōs **ka**-mas kon **doo**-cha?*
Do you have a double room with bath?	¿Tiene una habitación doble con baño? ***tyay**-nay **oo**-na a-bee-tath-**yon** do-blay kon **ban**-yō?*
I want to stay for 3 nights	Quiero quedarme tres noches ***kyay**-rō kay-**dar**-may tres **no**-chays*
We shall be staying until the sixth of May	Nos quedaremos hasta el seis de Mayo *nos kay-da-**ray**-mōs **as**-ta el se-ees day **ma**-yō*
How much is the room per night?	¿Cuánto es la habitación por noche? ***kwan**-tō es la a-bee-tath-**yon** por **no**-chay?*
Is that inclusive?	¿Todo incluido? ***tō**-dō een-kloo-**ee**-dō?*
How much is half-board?	¿Cuánto es con media pensión? ***kwan**-tō es kon **med**-ya pen-**syon**?*
How much is full board?	¿Cuánto es con pensión completa? ***kwan**-tō es kon pen-**syon** kom-**play**-ta?*
Do you have a cot (crib) for our baby?	¿Tienen una cuna para el niño? ***tyay**-nen **oo**-na **koo**-na **pa**-ra el **neen**-yō?*
Where can I park the car?	¿Dónde puedo aparcar el coche? ***don**-day **pway**-dō a-par-**kar** el **ko**-chay?*

Hotels

What time is ¿A qué hora es *a kay ō-ra es*	**– breakfast** el desayuno? *el des-a-yoo-nō?*
	– lunch · la comida? *la ko-mee-da?*
	– dinner la cena? *la thay-na?*
Can we have breakfast in our room, please?	¿Pueden servirnos el desayuno en la habitación, por favor? *pway-den ser-beer-nōs el des-a-yoo-nō en la a-bee-tath-yon, por fa-bor?*
What time does the hotel close?	¿A qué hora cierra el hotel? *a kay ō-ra thye-rra el ō-tel?*
Is there a lift (elevator)?	¿Hay ascensor? *a-ee as-then-sor?*
Can I drink the tap-water?	¿Se puede beber el agua del grifo? *say pway-day be-ber el a-gwa del gree-fō?*
Please call me at 8 o'clock	Despiérteme a las ocho, por favor *des-pyer-tay-may a las o-chō, por fa-bor*
Can I leave these for safe-keeping?	¿Puedo dejar esto en la caja fuerte? *pway-dō day-khar es-tō en la ka-kha fwer-tay?*
Can I have my things back from the safe?	¿Pueden devolverme las cosas que dejé en la caja fuerte? *pway-den day-bol-ber-may las kō-sas kay day-khay en la ka-kha fwer-tay?*
Can I make a telephone call from here?	¿Puedo llamar por teléfono desde aquí? *pway-dō lya-mar por tay-lay-fo-nō des-day a-kee?*
Is the voltage 220 or 110?	¿La corriente es de 220 o de 110? *la ko-rryen-tay es day dōs-thyen-tōs be-een-tay o day thyen-tō dyeth?*
Where is the bathroom?	¿Dónde está el cuarto de baño? *don-day e-sta el kwar-tō day ban-yō?*

Can I have – **my key please?**
¿Puede darme la llave, por favor?
pway-day dar-may *la **lya**-bay, por fa-bor?*

– **some coat hangers?**
unas perchas?
oo nas per-chas?

– **an ashtray**
un cenicero
*oon thay-nee-**thay**-rō?*

– **some note paper?**
papel de escribir?
*pa-**pel** day es-kree-beer?*

– **another blanket?**
otra manta?
*ō-tra **man**-ta?*

– **another pillow?**
otra almohada?
*ō-tra al-mō-**a**-da?*

Where is the socket (outlet) – ¿Dónde hay un enchufe para la
for my razor? máquina de afeitar?
*don-day a-ee oon en-**choo**-fay **pa**-ra la ma-**kee**-na day a-fe-ee-**tar**?*

There are no towels in the – No tengo toalla en la habitación
room *no **teng**-gō tō-**a**-lya en la a-bee-tath-**yon***

The room is too noisy – La habitación es demasiado ruidosa
*la a-bee-tath-**yon** es day-mas-**ya**-dō rwee-**dō**-sa*

The light is not working – La luz no funciona
*la looth nō foong-**thyo**-na*

The air-conditioning is not – El aire acondicionado no funciona
working *el **a**-ee-ray a-kon-deeth-yo-na-dō nō foong-**thyo**-na*

I cannot open the window – No puedo abrir la ventana
*nō **pway**-dō a-**breer** la ben-ta-na*

The heating is not working – La calefacción no funciona
*la ka-lay-fak-**thyon** nō foong-**thyo**-na*

Hotels

I cannot turn the heating off –	No puedo apagar la calefacción *nō **pway**-dō a-pa-**gar** la ka-lay-fak-**thyon***
The lock is broken –	La cerradura está rota *la thay-rra-**doo**-ra es-**ta rō**-ta*
There is no hot water –	No hay agua caliente *no **a**-ee **a**-gwa kal-**yen**-tay*
The washbasin is dirty –	El lavabo está sucio *el la-**ba**-bō es-**ta sooth**-yō*
There is no plug in the washbasin –	No hay tapón en el lavabo *nō **a**-ee ta-**pon** en el la-**ba**-bō*
There is no toilet paper –	No hay papel higiénico *nō **a**-ee pa-**pel** ee-**khyen**-ee-kō*
Do you have a laundry room? –	¿Tienen lavandería? ***tyay**-nen la-ban-day-**ree**-a?*
I want to iron some clothes –	Quiero planchar unas cosas ***kyay**-rō plan-**char** oo-nas **ko**-sas*
I want to stay an extra night –	Quiero quedarme otra noche ***kyay**-rō kay-**dar**-may **ō**-tra **no**-chay*
We will be leaving tomorrow at 9 o'clock –	Nos marchamos mañana a las nueve *nōs mar-**cha**-mōs man-**ya**-na a las **nway**-bay*
I would like the bill please –	La factura, por favor *la fak-**too**-ra, por fa-**bor***
Do you accept traveller's cheques? –	¿Aceptan cheques de viaje? *a-**thep**-tan **che**-kays day **bya**-khay?*
Could you have my luggage brought down? –	¿Podrían bajarme el equipaje? *po-**dree**-an ba-**khar**-may el ay-kee-**pa**-khay?*
Can you order me a taxi? –	¿Puede llamarme un taxi? ***pway**-day lya-**mar**-may oon **tak**-see?*
Thank you, we enjoyed our stay –	Gracias, ha sido una estancia muy agradable ***grath**-yas, a **see**-dō **oo**-na es-**tanth**-ya mwee a-gra-**da**-blay*

If you're a typical absent-minded visitor you will probably leave something behind when you go home. This letter may help you get it back if you copy it out carefully. Of course you will have to find out for yourself the Spanish for the missing item and insert it after '*dejado*'.

Dear Sirs,

I recently spent some time in your hotel in room 16. I believe I forgot

a pair of shoes

when I left. If you would be good enough to send them on to me I would be most grateful and refund the cost of postage.

Yours faithfully,

Estimados señores,

Me he hospedado recientemente en su hotel en la habitación número 16. Creo haberme dejado

un par de zapatos

al marchar. Si tuviera la amabilidad de enviármelos le estaría muy agradecido y le abonaría los gastos de envío.

Atentamente,

Rented Villas

This kind of holiday is increasingly popular, so we hope this section will help you settle in to your home from home.

We have arranged to rent a house	Hemos contratado el alquiler de una casa *ay-mōs kon-tra-ta-dō el al-kee-ler day oo-na ka-sa*
Here is our booking	Aquí está el contrato *a-kee es-ta el kon-tra-tō*
We need 2 sets of keys	Necesitamos dos juegos de llaves *nay-thay-see-ta-mōs dōs khway-gōs day lya-bays*
Will you show us round?	¿Nos enseña la casa, por favor? *nōs en-sayn-ya la ka-sa, por fa-bor*
Which is the key for this door?	¿Cuál es la llave de esta puerta? *kwal es la lya-bay day es-ta pwer-ta?*
Where are the fuses?	¿Dónde están los plomos? *don-day es-tan lōs plō-mōs?*
Where is the water heater?	¿Dónde está el calentador del agua? *don-day es-ta el ka-len-ta-dor del a-gwa?*
Please show us how this works	Enséñemos cómo funciona esto, por favor *en-sayn-yay-nōs kō-mō foong-thyo-na es-tō, por fa-bor*
How does the heating work?	¿Cómo funciona la calefacción? *kō-mō foong-thyo-na la ka-lay-fak-thyon?*
When does the help come?	¿Cuándo vendrán a ayudar? *kwan-dō ben-dran a a-yoo-dar?*
Is there any spare bedding?	¿Tiene más cubiertas? *tyay-nay mas koo-byer-tas?*
Can I contact you if there are any problems?	¿Puedo ponerme en contacto con usted si hay algún problema? *pway-dō po-ner-may en kon-tak-tō kon oos-ted see a-ee al-goon pro-blay-ma?*
The cooker (stove) does not work	La cocina no funciona *la ko-thee-na nō foong-thyo-na*

Rented Villas

I can't open the windows – No puedo abrir las ventanas
*nō **pway**-dō a-**breer** las ben-**ta**-nas*

We can't get any water – No tenemos agua
*nō tay-**nay**-mōs **a**-gwa*

The toilet won't flush – La cisterna no funciona
*la thees-**ter**-na nō foong-**thyo**-na*

A fuse has blown – Se han fundido los plomos
*say an foon-**dee**-dō lōs **plō**-mōs*

There is a gas leak – Hay un escape de gas
*a-ee oon es-**ka**-pay day gas*

I need somebody to fix this – Necesito a alguien que arregle estó
*nay-thay-**see**-tō a **alg**-yen kay a-**rray**-glay
es-tō*

bath	bañera *ban-**yay**-ra*	**pan**	cacerola *ka-thay- **rō**-la*
bathroom	cuarto de baño *kwar-tō day **ban**-yō*	**plate**	plato *pla-tō*
bed	cama *ka-ma*	**refrigerator**	frigorífico *free-go-**ree**-fee-kō*
brush	cepillo *thay-**peel**-yō*	**sheet**	sábana *sa-ba-na*
can opener	abrelatas *a-bray-**la**-tas*	**sink**	fregadero *fray-ga-**day**-rō*
chair	silla *seel-ya*	**spoon**	cuchara *koo-**cha**-ra*
cooker	cocina *ko-**thee**-na*	**stove**	cocina *koo-**thee**-na*
corkscrew	sacacorchos *sa-ka-**kor**-chōs*	**table**	mesa *may-sa*
fork	tenedor *tay-nay-**dor***	**tap**	grifo *gree-fō*
glass	vaso *ba-sō*	**toilet**	water *ba-ter*
kitchen	cocina *ko-**thee**-na*	**vacuum cleaner**	aspirador *a-spee-ra-**dor***
knife	cuchillo *koo-**cheel**-yō*	**washbasin**	lavabo *la-ba-bō*

Travelling with a Family

If you take the family away with you, anything can happen and probably will, but these phrases should be useful in at least some of the situations you'll encounter.

There are four of us	Somos cuatro *sō-mōs **kwa**-trō*
my wife	mi mujer *mee moo-**kher***
my husband	mi marido *mee ma-**ree**-dō*
my daughter	mi hija *mee **ee**-kha*
my son	mi hijo *mee **ee**-khō*
Have you got a cot (crib) for our baby?	¿Tiene una cuna para el niño? *tyay-nay oo-na **koo**-na **pa**-ra el neen-yō?*
Can my son sleep in our room?	¿Puede dormir nuestro hijo en nuestra habitación? ***pway**-day dor-**meer** nwes-trō ee-khō en nwes-tra a-bee-tath-**yon**?*
Are there any other children in the hotel?	¿Hay mas niños en el hotel? *a-ee mas neen-yōs en el ō-**tel**?*
How old are your children?	¿Qué edad tienen sus niños? *kay ay-**dad** tyay-nen soos neen-yōs?*
The boy is 9 years old	El niño tiene nueve años *el neen-yō tyay-nay **nway**-bay an-yōs*
The girl is 15 months	La niña tiene quince meses *la **neen**-ya tyay-nay **keen**-thay **may**-says*
Where can I feed my baby?	¿Dónde puedo darle el pecho al niño? ***don**-day **pway**-dō **dar**-lay el **pay**-chō al neen-yō?*
Can you warm this bottle for me?	¿Podría calentarme este biberón, por favor? *po-**dree**-a ka-len-**tar**-may es-tay bee-bay-**ron,** por fa-**bor**?*

Travelling with a Family

I need some disposable nappies (diapers) — Necesito pañales disponibles
*nay-thay-**see**-tō pan-**ya**-lays dees-po-**nee**-blays*

Have you got a highchair? — ¿Tiene una silla alta de niño?
***tyay**-nay **oo**-na **seel**-ya **al**-ta day **neen**-yō?*

Do you know anyone who will babysit for us? — ¿Conoce a alguien que pueda cuidarnos a los niños?
*ko-**no**-thay a **al**-gyen kay **pway**-da kwee-**dar**-nōs a los **neen**-yōs?*

We will be back at 11 — Volveremos a las once
*bol-bay-**ray**-mōs a las **on**-thay*

She goes to bed at 8 — Se acuesta a las ocho
*say a-**kwes**-ta a las **o**-chō*

Are there any organized activities for the children? — ¿Hay actividades organizadas para los niños?
*a-ee ak-tee-bee-**da**-days or-ga-nee-**tha**-das **pa**-ra lōs **neen**-yōs?*

Is there a paddling pool? — ¿Hay un estanque de juegos?
*a-ee oon es-**tan**-kay day **khway**-gōs?*

Is there an amusement park? — ¿Hay parque de atracciones?
*a-ee **par**-kay day a-trak-**thyo**-nays?*

Is there a zoo nearby? — ¿Hay algún zoológico cerca?
*a-ee al-**goon** tho-o-**lo**-khee-kō **ther**-ka?*

My son has hurt himself — Mi hijo se ha hecho daño
*mee **ee**-khō say a **ay**-chō **dan**-yō*

My daughter is ill — Mi hija está enferma
*mee **ee**-kha es-**ta** en-**fer**-ma*

I'm very sorry. That was very naughty of him — Lo siento mucho. Es terrible que haya hecho eso
*lō **syen**-tō **moo**-chō. es tay-**rree**-blay kay a-ya **ay**-chō e-sō*

Camping

There are a great number of officially recognised camping sites in Spain, especially along the Mediterranean coast, and many of them have good facilities. If you can't find an official site, however, landowners will often allow you to camp on their property.

Is there anywhere for us to camp near here?	– ¿Hay algún sitio para acampar cerca de aquí? *a-ee al-**goon** seet-yō **pa**-ra a-kam-**par** ther-ka day a-kee?*
Do you have a site for our tent?	– ¿Tiene un sitio para nuestra tienda? *tyay-nay oon **seet**-yō pa-ra **nwes**-tra **tyen**-da?*
Do you mind if we camp on your land?	– ¿Le importa que acampemos en su terreno? *lay eem-**por**-ta kay a-kam-**pay**-mōs en soo tay-**rray**-nō?*
May we pitch our tent here?	– ¿Podemos poner la tienda aquí? *po-**day**-mōs po-**ner** la **tyen**-da a-kee?*
This site is very muddy	– Este sitio tiene mucho barro *es-tay **seet**-yō tyay-nay **moo**-chō **ba**-rrō*
Could we have a more sheltered site?	– ¿Tienen algún sitio mas abrigado? *tyay-nen al-**goon** seet-yō mas a-bree-**ga**-dō?*
Can we put our caravan (trailer) here?	– ¿Podemos estacionar la caravana aquí? *po-**day**-mōs es-tath-yo-**nar** la ka-ra-**ba**-na a-kee?*
Is there a shop on the site?	– ¿Hay alguna tienda en el camping? *a-ee al-**goo**-na **tyen**-da en el **kam**-peeng?*
Can I have a shower?	– ¿Puedo ducharme? ***pway**-dō doo-**char**-may?*
Where is the drinking water?	– ¿Dónde está el agua potable? ***don**-day es-ta el **ag**-wa po-**ta**-blay?*
Where are the toilets and washroom?	– ¿Dónde están los servicios y los lavabos? ***don**-day es-**tan** lōs ser-**beeth**-yōs ee lōs la-ba-bōs?*

Camping

Where can we wash our dishes?	– ¿Dónde podemos lavar los platos? *don*-day po-*day*-mōs la-*bar* lōs **pla**-tōs?
Is there another camp-site near here?	– ¿Hay algún otro camping cerca de aquí? *a-ee* al-**goon** ō-trō **kam**-*peeng* **ther**-ka day *a*-**kee**?

air mattress	colchón hinchable kol-**chon** een-**cha**-blay		**guy line**	viento **byen**-tō
back pack	mochila mo-**chee**-la		**knife**	cuchillo koo-**cheel**-yō
bottle opener	abrebotellas a-bray-bo-**tayl**-yas		**mallet**	mazo **ma**-thō
bucket	cubo **koo**-bō		**matches**	cerillas thay-**reel**-yas
camp bed	cama de camping **ka**-ma day **kam**-peeng		**pail**	cubo **koo**-bō
camp chair	silla de camping **seel**-ya day **kam**-peeng		**penknife**	navaja na-**ba**-kha
candle	vela **bay**-la		**plate**	plato **pla**-tō
can opener	abrelatas a-bray-**la**-tas		**rucksack**	mochila mo-**chee**-la
cup	taza **ta**-tha		**shelter**	refugio ray-**foo**-khyō
fire	fuego **fway**-gō		**sleeping bag**	saco de dormir **sa**-kō day dor-**meer**
flashlight	linterna leen-**ter**-na		**spoon**	cuchara koo-**cha**-ra
fly sheet	doble techo **do**-blay **tay**-chō		**stove**	hornillo or-**neel**-yō
folding table	mesa plegable **may**-sa play-ga-blay		**tent pegs**	clavijas (de la tienda) kla-**bee**-khas (day la **tyen**-da)
fork	tenedor tay-nay-**dor**		**tent pole**	mástil **mas**-teel
frying pan	sartén sar-**ten**		**thermos flask**	termo **ter**-mō
ground	suelo **sway**-lō		**torch**	linterna leen-**ter**-na

Youth Hostels

Here is my international membership card	– Aquí está mi carnet internacional de alberguista *a-**kee** es-**ta** mee **kar**-nay* *een-ter-nath-yo-**nal** day al-ber-**gees**-ta*
How long can I stay?	– ¿Cuánto tiempo me puedo quedar? *kwan-tō **tyem**-pō may **pway**-dō kay-**dar**?*
I want to stay two nights here	– Quiero quedarme dos noches aquí *kyay-rō kay-**dar**-may dōs **no**-chays a-**kee***
I would like to join here	– Quiero hacerme miembro aquí *kyay-rō a-**ther**-may **myem**-brō a-**kee***
Are you open during the day?	– ¿Está abierto durante el día? *es-**ta** a-**byer**-tō doo-**ran**-tay el **dee**-a?*
What time do you close?	– ¿A qué hora cierran? *a kay ō-ra **thyer**-rran?*
Do you serve meals?	– ¿Sirven comidas? *seer-ben ko-**mee**-das?*
Can I use the kitchen?	– ¿Puedo utilizar la cocina? *pway-dō oo-tee-lee-**thar** la ko-**thee**-na?*
I want to rent a sheet for my sleeping bag	– Quiero alquilar una sábana para mi saco de dormir *kyay-rō al-kee-**lar** oo-na **sa**-ba-na **pa**-ra mee **sa**-kō day dor-**meer***
Is there another youth hostel near here?	– ¿Hay algún otro albergue juvenil cerca de aquí? *a-ee al-**goon** ō-trō al-**ber**-gay khoo-bay-**neel** **ther**-ka day a-**kee**?*

Churches

Where is there – ¿Dónde hay *don-day a-ee*	**a Catholic church?** una iglesia católica? *oo-na ee-glay-sya ka-to-lee-ka?*
–	**a Protestant church?** une iglesia protestante? *oo-na ee-glay-sya pro-tes-tan-tay?*
–	**a Baptist church?** une iglesia baptista? *oo-na ee-glay-sya bap-tees-ta?*
–	**a synagogue?** una sinagoga? *oo-na see-na-go-ga?*
–	**a mosque?** una mezquita? *oo-na meth-kee-ta?*
What time is the service?	¿A qué hora son los oficios? *a kay ō-ra son los ō-feeth-yōs?*
I'd like to see – Quería hablar con *kay-ree-a a-blar con*	**a priest . . .** un sacerdote . . . *oon sa-ther-do-tay . . .*
–	**a minister . . .** un pastor . . . *oon pas-tor . . .*
–	**a rabbi . . .** un rabino . . . *oon ra-bee-nō*
. . . who speaks English –	. . . que hable inglés *kay a-blay eeng-glays*
What will the choir be **singing?** –	¿Qué va a cantar el coro? *kay ba a kan-tar el kō-rō?*

The Weather

You may need to know the weather forecast, or you may just want to make conversation . . .

It's a lovely day isn't it?	Hace un día estupendo, ¿verdad? *a-thay oon **dee**-a es-too-**pen**-dō, ber-**dad**?*
It's too hot for me	Para mí hace demasiado calor ***pa**-ra mee a-thay day-ma-**sya**-dō ka-**lor***
There's a nice breeze	Hace una brisa muy agradable *a-thay oo-na **bree**-sa mwee a-gra-**da**-blay*
It's raining	Está lloviendo *es-ta lyō-**byen**-dō*
It's windy	Hace viento *a-thay **byen**-tō*
It's snowing	Está nevando *es-**ta** nay-**ban**-dō*
It's foggy	Hay niebla *a-nee **nyay**-bla*
It's cold	Hace frío *a-thay **free**-ō*
Is it going ¿Va a *ba a*	**to be fine?** hacer buen tiempo? *a-**ther** bwen **tyem**-pō?*
	– to rain? llover? *lyo-**ber**?*
	– to be windy? hacer viento? *a-**ther byen**-tō?*
	– to snow? nevar? *nay-**bar**?*
What is the temperature?	¿Qué temperatura hace? *kay tem-pay-ra-**too**-ra a-thay?*
Is it going to stay like this?	¿Va a seguir así? *ba a say-**geer** a-see?*

The Weather

Will the weather improve?	– ¿Mejorará el tiempo? *may-kho-ra-**ra** el **tyem**-pō?*
Is it going to get any cooler?	– ¿Refrescará algo el tiempo? *ray-fres-ka-**ra al**-gō el **tyem**-pō?*
Will the wind go down?	– ¿Se calmará el viento? *say kal-ma-**ru** el **byen**-tō?*
Is there going to be a thunderstorm?	– ¿Va a haber tormenta? *ba a a-**ber** tor-**men**-ta?*
Is the sea calm?	– ¿Está el mar en calma? *es-**ta** el mar en **kal**-ma?*
Is the water warm?	– ¿Está el agua caliente? *es-**ta** el **a**-gwa kal-**yen**-tay?*
When is high tide?	– ¿Cuándo está la marea alta? ***kwan**-dō es-**ta** la ma-**ray**-a **al**-ta?*
It's a clear night	– Hace una noche muy clara ***a**-thay **oo**-na **no**-chay mwee **kla**-ra*
Will it be cold tonight?	– ¿Hará frío esta noche? *a-**ra** free-ō es-ta **no**-chay?*
The stars are out	– El cielo está estrellado *el **thyay**-lō es-**ta** es-trel-**ya**-dō*

Leisure & Entertainment
On the Beach

A red flag on a Spanish beach means that it is dangerous to go swimming. A yellow flag means that you can swim, but it is not recommended. If you see a green flag, it means you can go right ahead!

Is it safe to swim here?	– ¿Se puede nadar sin peligro aquí? *say **pway**-day na-**dar** seen pay-lee-grō a-**kee**?*
Is this a private beach?	– ¿Es privada esta playa? *es pree-**ba**-da **es**-ta **pla**-ya?*
Can you recommend a quiet beach?	– ¿Puede recomendarme una playa tranquila? ***pway**-day ray-ko-men-**dar**-may **oo**-na **pla**-ya trang-**kee**-la?*
Where can we change?	– ¿Dónde podemos cambiarnos? ***don**-day po-**day**-mōs kam-**byar**-nōs?*

Can I rent
¿Puedo alquilar
pway-dō al-kee-lar

– **a deck chair?**
una silla de playa?
oo-na seel-ya day pla-ya?

– **a sunshade?**
una sombrilla?
oo-na som-breel-ya?

– **a sailing boat?**
un barco de vela?
oon bar-kō day bay-la?

Is it possible to go
¿Se puede
say pway-day

– **sailing?**
navegar a vela?
na-bay-gar a bay-la?

– **water-skiing?**
hacer esquí acuático?
a-ther e-skee a-kwa-tee-kō?

– **surfing?**
hacer surfing?
a-ther soor-feeng?

– **wind surfing?**
hacer surfing a vela?
a-ther soor-feeng a bay-la?

Leisure & Entertainment
Outdoors & Night Life

Is there –	**a swimming pool?**
¿Hay	piscina?
a-ee	*pees-**thee**-na?*
	– **a tennis court?**
	pista de tenis?
	pees-ta day te-nees?
	– **a golf course?**
	campo de golf?
	kam-pō day golf?

Is it possible to go riding? – ¿Se puede montar a caballo?
*say **pway**-day mon-**tar** ā ka-**bal**-yō?*

Can I go fishing? – ¿Puedo ir a pescar?
pway**-dō eer a pes-**kar?

Can I rent the equipment? – ¿Puedo alquilar el equipo?
***pway**-dō al-kee-**lar** el ay-kee-pō?*

Do you know any interesting walks? – ¿Sabe de alguna ruta interesante para caminar?
*sa-bay day al-**goo**-na **roo**-ta een-tay-ray-**san**-tay **pa**-ra ka-mee-**nar?***

Are there any local festivals nearby? – ¿Hay alguna fiesta local por aquí cerca?
*a-ee al-**goo**-na **fyes**-ta lō-**kal** por a-**kee ther**-ka?*

Are there any films in English? – ¿Hay alguna película en inglés?
*a-ee al-**goo**-na pay-**lee**-koo-la en eeng-**glays?***

Is there a concert? – ¿Hay concierto?
*a-ee kon-**thyer**-tō?*

2 balcony tickets, please – Dos entradas de palco, por favor
*dōs en-**tra**-das day **pal**-kō, por fa-**bor***

2 stalls (orchestra) tickets, please – Dos entradas de butaca, por favor
*dōs en-**tra**-das day boo-**ta**-ka, por fa-**bor***

Are there any good night-clubs? – ¿Hay algún club nocturno bueno?
*a-ee al-**goon** kloob nok-**toor**-nō **bway**-nō?*

Is there a disco? – ¿Hay discoteca?
*a-ee dees-kō-**tay**-ka?*

Sightseeing

What is there to see here?	¿Qué hay aquí interesante para ver? *kay a-ee a-kee een-tay-ray-san-tay pa-ra ber?*
Have you got a town guide?	¿Tiene una guía de la cuidad? *tyay-nay oo-na gee-a day la thyoo-dad?*
What is this building?	¿Qué es este edificio? *kay es es-tay ay-dee-feeth-yō?*
When was it built?	¿Cuando se construyó? *kwan-dō say kon-stroo-yō?*
Is it open to the public?	¿Está abierto al público? *es-ta ab-yer-tō al poo-blee-kō?*
Are there any sightseeing tours?	¿Hay excursiones turísticas? *a-ee ek-skoor-syo-nays too-ree-stee-kas?*
Is there a tour of the castle?	¿Hay visitas organizadas al castillo? *a-ee bee-see-tas or-ga-nee-tha-das al kas-teel-yō?*
How long does the tour take?	¿Cuánto dura la visita? *kwan-tō doo-ra la bee-see-ta?*
Are there any guided tours of the cathedral?	¿Hay visitas con guía a la catedral? *a-ee bee-see-tas kon gee-a a la ka-tay-dral?*
Is there an English-speaking guide?	¿Hay un guía que hable inglés? *a-ee oon gee-a kay a-blay eeng-glays?*
Have you got an English guidebook?	¿Tiene una guía en inglés? *tyay-nay oo-na gee-a en een-glays?*
What time does the museum open?	¿A qué hora abre el museo? *a kay ō-ra a-bray el moo-say-ō?*
Can we go in?	¿Podemos entrar? *po-day-mōs en-trar?*
Are these monuments illuminated at night?	¿Están iluminados estos monumentos por la noche? *e-stan ee-loo-mee-na-dōs es-tōs mo-noo-men-tōs por la no-chay?*
What is the admission charge?	¿Cuánto cuesta la entrada? *kwan-tō kwes-ta la en-tra-da?*

Sightseeing

Can we go up to the top? –	¿Podemos subir hasta arriba? *po-**day**-mōs soo-**beer** as-ta a-**rree**-ba?*
Where is the best view? –	¿Desde dónde hay mejor vista? ***des**-day **don**-day a-ee may-**khor** bees-ta?*
Can I take photos? –	¿Puedo hacer fotos? ***pway**-dō a-**ther** fō-tōs?*
Can I use a flash? –	¿Puedo usar el flash? ***pway**-dō oo-**sar** el flash?*
Have you got any postcards? –	¿Tiene tarjetas postales? ***tyay**-nay tar-**khay**-tas pos-ta-lays?*
Have you got any colour slides? –	¿Tiene diapositivas en color? ***tyan**-nay dee-a-po-see-**tee**-bas en ko-**lor**?*
Where can you buy souvenirs? –	¿Dónde podemos comprar recuerdos? ***don**-day po-**day**-mōs kom-**prar** ray-**kwer**-dōs?*
Would you take a photo of us, please? –	¿Puede hacernos una foto, por favor? ***pway**-day a-**ther**-nōs oo-na fō-tō, por fa-**bor**?*

Eating & Drinking
Restaurants

Spain has much to offer lovers of good food. You can have memorable meals all over the country, in elegant city restaurants or in local inns (*fondas*). Set price menus are usually good value, but beware of *menús turísticos* in places obviously catering for tourists, where the standards are not likely to be high for customers who are only passing through. The best recommendation is the presence of the Spanish themselves. The menu-reader on page 64 will help you decide what to eat – don't miss the opportunity to sample local specialities.

Can we have a table for two?	–	Una mesa para dos, por favor *oo-na **may**-sa **pa**-ra dōs, por fa-**bor***
Can I reserve a table for four at 8 o'clock?	–	¿Puedo reservar une mesa para cuatro a las ocho? ***pway**-dō ray-ser-**bar** oo-na **may**-sa **pa**-ra **kwa**-trō a las o-chō?*
We'd like a table Querríamos una mesa *kay-**rree**-a-amōs oo-na **may**-sa*	–	**by the window** junto a la ventana ***khoon**-tō a la ben-**ta**-na*
	–	**on the terrace** en la terraza *en la te-**rra**-tha*
The menu please	–	La carta, por favor *la **kar**-ta, por fa-**bor***
Do you have a set menu?	–	¿Tienen plato del día? ***tyay**-nen **pla**-tō del **dee**-a?*
I will take the set menu	–	Tráigame el plato del día *tra-ee-ga-may el **pla**-tō del **dee**-a*
We will take the menu at 500 pesetas	–	Tráiganos el plato del día de quinientas pesetas *tra-ee-ga-nōs el **pla**-tō del **dee**-a de keen-**yen**-tas pay-**say**-tas*
Is this good?	–	¿Está bueno esto? *es-**ta bway**-nō es-tō?*
What is this dish like?	–	¿Cómo es este plato? ***kō**mō es **es**-tay **pla**-tō?*

Eating & Drinking
Restaurants

What do you recommend?	— ¿Qué nos recomienda? *kay nōs ray-kom-**yen**-da?*
Do you have a local speciality?	— ¿Tiene algúna especialidad local? *tyay-nay al-**goo**-na es-peth-ya-lee-**dad** lo-**kal**?*
I'll take that	— Tráigame eso *tra-ee-ga-may e-sō*
We will begin with onion soup	— Empezaremos con sopa de cebolla *em-pay-tha-**ray**-mōs kon **sō**-pa day thay-**bol**-ya*
I will have steak and chips (French fries)	— Tráigame un filete con patatas fritas *tra-ee-ga-may oon fee-**lay**-tay kon pa-ta-tas **free**-tas*
I like it Me gusta *may **goos**-ta*	**very rare** muy poco pasado *mwee **pō**-kō pa-**sa**-dō*
	— **rare** poco pasado ***pō**-kō pa-**sa**-dō*
	— **medium rare** medianamente pasado *mayd-ya-na-**men**-tay pa-**sa**-dō*
	— **well done** bien pasado *byen pa-**sa**-dō*
Are vegetables included?	— ¿Incluye vegetales? *en-**kloo**-yay bay-khay-**ta**-les?*
Is this cheese very strong?	— ¿Es muy fuerte este queso? *es mwee **fwer**-tay **es**-tay kay-sō?*
That is for me	— Eso es para mí *e-sō es **pa**-ra mee*
That is for over here	— Eso es para aquí *e-sō es **pa**-ra a-**kee***
How do I eat this?	— ¿Cómo se come esto? ***kō**-mō say ko-may es-tō?*

Eating & Drinking
Restaurants

Could we have some more bread please?	– ¿Nos puede traer más pan, por favor? *nōs **pway**-day tra-er mas pan, por fa-**bor**?*
Could I have some butter?	– ¿Me puede traer mantequilla? *may **pway**-day tra-er man-tay-**keel**-ya?*
What is this called?	– ¿Cómo se llama esto? *kō-mō say **lya**-ma es-tō?*
Would you bring another glass please?	– ¿Puede traernos otro vaso, por favor? ***pway**-day tra-er-nōs ō-trō **ba**-sō, por fa-**bor**?*
That is not what I ordered	– Eso no es lo que pedí *e-sō nō es lō kay pay-**dee***
This is very salty	– Esto está muy salado *es-tō es-**ta** mwee sa-**la**-dō*
I wanted cheese	– Quería queso *kay **ree**-a **kay**-sō*
Have you forgotten the soup?	– ¿Se ha olvidado de la sopa? *sa a ol-bee-**da**-dō day la **sō**-pa?*
This is cold	– Esto está frío *es-tō es-**ta free**-ō*
This is very good	– Esto está muy bueno *es-tō es-**ta** mwee **bway**-nō*
I'll have a dessert please	– Voy a tomar postre, por favor *boy a tō-**mar pos**-tray, por fa-**bor***
The wine list please	– La carta de vinos, por favor *la **kar**-ta day bee-nōs, por fa-**bor***
Which wine do you recommend?	– ¿Qué vino recomienda usted? *kay **bee**-nō ray-kom-**yen**-da oos-**ted**?*
Is the local wine good?	– ¿Es bueno el vino del país? *es **bway**-nō el bee-nō del pa-**ees**?*
We'll take the Rioja	– Tráiganos un Rioja ***tra**-ee-ga-nōs oon ree-ō-kha*
A jug of red wine	– Una jarra de vino tinto ***oo**-na **kha**-rra day bee-nō **teen**-tō*
A bottle of white wine	– Una botella de vino blanco ***oo**-na bo-**tel**-ya day bee-nō **blang**-kō*

Eating & Drinking
Restaurants

Another bottle please – Otra botella, por favor
*ō-tra bo-**tel**-ya, por fa-**bor***

Some plain water please – Una jarra de agua, por favor
*oo-na **kha**-rra day a-**gwa**, por fa-**bor***

Some mineral water, please – Un agua mineral, por favor
*oon a-gwa mee-nay-**ral**, por fa-**bor***

A beer please – Una cerveza, por favor
*oo-na ther-**bay**-tha, por fa-**bor***

Black coffee, please – Un café solo, por favor
*oon ka-**fay** sō-lō, por fa-**bor***

Coffee with milk, please – Un café con leche, por favor
*oon ka-**fay** kon **lay**-chay, por fa-**bor***

We're in a hurry – Tenemos prisa
*tay-**nay**-mos **pree**-sa*

The bill please – La cuenta, por favor
*la **kwen**-ta, por fa-**bor***

Is service included? – ¿Incluye el servicio?
*een-**kloo**-yay el ser-**beeth**-yō?*

There's a mistake here – Hay un error aquí
*a-ee oon e-**rror** a-**kee***

The meal was excellent – Ha sido una comida excelente
*a **see**-do **oo**-na ko-**mee**-da eks-thay-**len**-tay*

Eating & Drinking
Menu Reader

We hope this menu reader will show how varied and appealing Spanish cookery can be, and enable you to choose each course with confidence.

Ajo de las manos (Patatas bravas)
Sliced, boiled potatoes mixed with a garlic, oil and vinegar dressing, and flavoured with red peppers

Albóndigas
Meat-ball rissoles

Alcachofas con jamón
Artichokes with ham

Almejas marinera
Steamed mussels/clams with a parsley, olive oil and garlic sauce

Angulas en cazuelita
Garlic flavoured, fried baby eels seasoned with hot pepper

Arroz blanco
Boiled rice

Arroz a la levantina
Rice with shellfish, onions, artichokes, peas, tomatoes and saffron

Arroz a la valenciana
The Valencian version of *Paella*. For this dish eel is usually added

Arroz a la zamorana
Rice with pork, peppers and flavoured with garlic (Leon)

Arroz con pollo
Rice with boiled chicken and garnished with peas and pimento (Cordoba)

Atún con salsa de tomate
Tuna fish with tomato sauce

Bacalao al ajo arriero
Dried cod fried with garlic to which is added vinegar, paprika and chopped parsley (Navarre)

Bacalao a la vizcaína
Fried dried cod with a tomato, pepper, onion and garlic purée

Bacalao con patatas
Dried cod slowly baked with potatoes, peppers, tomatoes, onions and olives and flavoured with a bayleaf (Cadiz)

Berenjenas rellenas
Stuffed aubergines

Berenjenas salteadas
Aubergines sautéd with tomatoes and onions

Boquerones fritos
Fried anchovies (Malaga)

Buñuelos
A brandy or rum flavoured batter filled with ham, mussel and prawn mixture. The whole deep fried and served piping hot

Butifarra con judías
Pork sausage with beans

Cachelos
Chopped boiled potatoes, boiled cabbage and garlic, red pepper and fried bacon. Often served with *chorizo* sausage and ham

Calabacines rellenos
Stuffed baby marrows

Eating & Drinking
Menu Reader

Calamares fritos
Fried squid or cuttlefish

Calamares a la romana
Squid fried in batter

Calamares en su tinta
Squid cooked in their ink

Caldeirada
Fish soup (Galicia)

Caldo
Clear soup or broth

Caldo gallego
Clear soup with green vegetables,
beans and pork (Galicia)

Caldo de pescado
Fish soup

Callos a la madrileña
Fried tripe casseroled in a spicy
paprika sauce with tomatoes and
chorizo sausage (Madrid)

Cebollas rellenas
Stuffed onions

Cerdo asado
Roast pork

Cochinillo asado
Roast suckling pig (Castile)

Cocido
Boiled chicken, meat and vegetable
stew. There are many different
regional variations of this dish and
it is worth trying the local *cocido*
wherever you are staying

Codornices asadas
Roast quail

Coliflor frita
Fried cauliflower

Consomé de gallina
Chicken consommé

Cordero asado
Roast lamb

Crema de tomate
Tomato soup

Croquetas de camarones
Shrimp croquettes

Empanadas de carne
Small meat and vegetable pies
which can be eaten hot or cold

Ensaladilla
Spanish version of Russian salad
(cooked cold vegetables mixed with
mayonnaise)

Escabeche de pescado
Fish marinated in oil and served
cold

Escalopes de ternera
Veal escalopes

Escudilla de pages
Dry white bean, sausage, ham and
pork soup (Catalonia)

Estofado de ternera/vaca
Veal/beef stew (Aragon &
Navarre)

Fabada
Pork, ham, black pudding, beans
and sausage stew. *Fabada* also can
vary from region to region. In
Asturias dried white haricot beans
are added

Faisán trufado
Truffled pheasant

Fiambre
Cold meat

Eating & Drinking
Menu Reader

Filetes de lenguado
Rolled sole baked with wine, mushrooms and butter (Madrid)

Gambas a la plancha
Grilled prawns

Gazpacho
This is the traditional cold soup of Spain and there are many varied recipes. Basically, however, it is water, tomatoes, onion, cucumber, green pepper, soft breadcrumbs, vinegar, oil, and seasoning. *Gazpacho* should always be served chilled with garnishes from the above ingredients. Some versions of this soup even have mayonnaise included in the ingredients

Gazpacho extremeña
A version of the soup made with finely chopped green peppers and onions, with these also served separately with the soup (Extremadura)

Guisantes con jamón a la española
Boiled peas with ham, lettuce, carrots and onions

Hígado con cebolla
Fried calf's liver with onions

Huevos a la española
Stuffed eggs with a cheese sauce

Huevos a la flamenca
Baked eggs with tomatoes, peas, peppers, asparagus and sausage (Seville)

Huevos al plato
Eggs baked in butter

Huevos revueltos con carne
Scrambled eggs with minced beef

Jamón de jabugo
An excellent Andalucian ham

Jamón serrano
Aromatic, dark red smoked ham

Judías verdes a la castellana/española
Boiled green beans mixed with fried parsley, garlic and pimentos (Castile)

Lacón con grelos
Shoulder of salted pork with young turnip tops and white cabbage hearts (Leon)

Langosta a la catalana
Potatoes with a lobster filling served with mayonnaise (Catalonia)

Langostinos a la vinagreta levantina
Casseroled crayfish with hard-boiled eggs and a cognac and vinaigrette sauce (Aragon)

Lenguados fritos
Fried fillets of sole often served on a bed of mixed sautéed vegetables

Lenguados rellenos
Fillets of sole stuffed with shrimps or prawns

Liebre estofada
Stewed hare (Castile)

Liebre estofada con judías
Hare stew with French beans

Menestra de legumbres
Braised spring vegetables

Eating & Drinking
Menu Reader

Menestra de legumbres frescas
Vegetable stew decorated with poached eggs and boiled asparagus (Murcia)

Merluza a la asturiana
Boiled hake served with mayonnaise and garnished with hard-boiled eggs, boiled potatoes and sometimes prawns (Asturias)

Merluza con sidra
Hake baked with clams, onions and cider

Moros y cristianos
Boiled rice, black beans and onions served with garlic sausage

Olla podrida
Ham vegetable and chick pea stew

Paella
One of the most famous of Spanish dishes. *Paella* varies from region to region but usually consists of rice, chicken, shellfish, vegetables, garlic and saffron. The dish derives its name from the large shallow pan in which it is cooked.

Paella de mariscos
A rice and shellfish *paella* (Valencia)

Paella a la valenciana
See *Arroz a la valenciana*

Patatas bravas
See *Ajo de las manos*

Patatas fritas
Chips (French Fries)

Pato a la sevillana
Joints of wild duck cooked with sherry, onion and tomatoes and flavoured with herbs and garlic, and served with oranges and olives in the sauce (Seville)

Pavo relleno
Stuffed turkey

Pechugas en bechamel
Chicken breasts in white sauce

Pepitoria de pavo/pollo
Turkey/chicken casserole (Cordoba)

Perdices de capellán
Rolled slices of fried veal, filled with ham and sausage (Balearic Islands)

Pimientos morrones
Pimento hors-d'oeuvre

Pimientos rellenos
Stuffed peppers (Asturias and Castile)

Pinchos morunos
Meat grilled on a skewer

Pisto
A mixture of sautéed peppers, onions, aubergines, tomatoes, garlic and parsley. Similar to the French *ratatouille*. Served cold

Pollo asado
Roast chicken

Pollo a la chilindrón
Chicken cooked with onion, ham, garlic, red peppers and tomatoes (Aragon)

Pollo a la pepitoria
Breaded chicken pieces fried, then casseroled with herbs, almonds, garlic and sherry

Eating & Drinking
Menu Reader

Pollo estofado
Chicken stewed with potatoes, button mushrooms, shallots, bayleaf and brandy

Pollo relleno
Stuffed chicken

Potaje madrileño
Vegetable soup (Madrid)

Potaje murciana
Red bean, French bean and rice soup (Murcia)

Pote gallego
Thick cabbage, white kidney bean, potato, pork and sausage soup (Galicia)

Puré de garbanzos
Thick chick pea soup

Puré leontino
Thick vegetable soup (Leon)

Quinad
Green vegetable stew with wild white peas and silver beet. A Good Friday speciality eaten in Ibiza

Riñones al jerez
Kidneys in sherry sauce (Andalucia)

Rustido a la catalana
Veal roasted with rum, herbs and white wine and flavoured with cinnamon and cloves (Catalonia)

Salchichas, chorizos y morcillas
Pork and spicy sausages and black pudding (Asturias)

Salchichón de Vich
Salami sausage (Catalonia)

Salmonete frito
Fried red mullet

Salmorejo
A type of *gazpacho* (Cordoba)

Sardinas frescas/fritas/rebozadas
Fresh sardines/fried/in batter

Sesos fritos
Fried brains

Sopa de ajo
Garlic soup (Madrid and Cadiz)

Sopa de ajo blanco
Cold grape or melon soup (Malaga)

Sopa de arroz
Rice soup

Sopa de cebolla
Onion soup

Sopa de mariscos
Shellfish soup

Sopa de pescado
Fish soup

Sopa de rape
Soup made with the mediterranean angler-fish, tomatoes, onions and nuts

Sopa de tomate
Tomato soup

Ternera asada con tomates rellenos
Roast veal with onion and sherry, served garnished with small stuffed tomatoes

Ternera fiambre
Veal paté

Eating & Drinking
Menu Reader

Ternera fría
Cold veal usually served in a sauce

Ternera rellena
Stuffed veal

Tomates rellenos
Stuffed tomatoes

Tortilla a la española
Traditional Spanish omelette made with potato, onion, garlic, tomato, peppers and seasoning

Tortilla con espárragos
Asparagus omelette

Tortilla con gambas
Prawn omelette (Seville)

Tortilla de habas
Broad bean omelette (Alicante)

Tortilla murciana
Tomato and pimento omelette (Murcia)

Tortilla de patatas
Potato omelette

Tortilla de sardinas frescas
Sardine omelette (Majorca)

Trucha a la navarra
Trout stuffed with ham slices (Navarre)

Trucha con jamón
Trout baked with ham and wine and served with a rasher of crisp fried bacon on each trout (Costa del Sol)

Zarzuela de mariscos
Seafood casserole

Zarzuela de pescado
Fish stew

Cheeses

Queso de bola
Cow's milk cheese similar to Dutch cheese

Queso de Burgos
Soft cheese from Castile

Queso de cabra
Goat's milk cheese

Queso fresco
Curd cheese

Queso manchego
Sheep's cheese from La Mancha

Queso de oveja
Sheep's cheese

Queso del país
Local cheese

Requesón
Curd cheese (Catalonia)

Rongal
Strong, dry cheese made from sheep's milk (Aragon and Navarre)

Eating & Drinking Menu Reader

Desserts

Arroz con leche
Cinnamon flavoured rice pudding (Andalusia)

Bizcocho borracho de Guadalajara
Sponge ring filled with brandy or rum, flavoured whipped cream and decorated with strawberries or glacé cherries. In Malaga, the speciality is bars of the sponge soaked in rum and topped with crisped, slightly browned meringue and served with cream

Cabello de ángel
Sugared pumpkin

Crema catalana
Cinnamon and lemon flavoured rich custard, topped with caramelized sugar (Catalonia)

Crema de chocolate
Chocolate cream

Cuajada
Junket (Valencia)

Flan (crema de caramelo)
The usual term for caramel cream

Flan de Pascuas
A mint and egg tart usually eaten during Easter (Balearic Islands)

Helado
Ice cream

Leche frita
Very thick custard dipped into an egg and breadcrumb mixture, fried and served hot in squares

Leche merengada
Milk and egg sorbet

Manzanas rellenas
Stuffed apples

Tocino de cielo
A rich caramel cream

Tortilla al ron
Sweet rum omelette

Tortilla soufflé
Sweet omelette soufflé

Tortitas
Pancakes

Turrones
Almond, beaten egg white and sugar sweet (Valencia)

Yemas
Beaten egg yolk and sugar dessert

Eating & Drinking
The Wine List

Amontillado
A medium sherry

Castellblanch
A fruity, sweet and sparkling wine

Chacolí
A slightly sour, red or white sparkling wine

Champana/Xampan
The Spanish version of champagne

Espumoso
Sparkling wine

Fino
The best, and driest, sherry

Fondillón
Dark red wine from Alicante

Jerez
Sherry – fortified wine from Jerez de la Frontera in Andalucia

Lágrima
The best Malaga wine

Málaga
Sweet, dark dessert wine from Malaga with a full, often muscat, flavour

Moscatel
Sweet wine made in many parts of Spain from muscat grapes

Ribeiro
Young, fresh wine from Orense

Rioja
Some of the best Spanish table wines, both red and white, from Castile

San Sadurní de Noya
Sparkling white wine from Panades

Sangría
Iced fruit punch

Valdepeñas
Red and white lightish wine from La Mancha

Vino blanco
White wine

Vino de la casa
The restaurant's house wine

Vino clarete
Light red wine

Vino común
Ordinary wine

Vino corriente
Draught wine

Vino dulce
Sweet wine

Vino espumoso
Sparkling wine

Vino generoso
Old and sweet wine

Vino de mesa
Table wine

Vino del país
Local wine

Vino rosado
Rosé wine

Vino seco
Dry wine

Vino tinto
Red wine

Vino tinto corriente
Red wine, locally produced and stored in barrels

Eating & Drinking
Bars & Cafés

Bars and cafés are an essential part of Spanish life, places where you can have breakfast, an apéritif, coffee after dinner, or just relax over a drink at any time of day. Many serve snacks and meals, and, of course, those delicious Spanish hors d'oeuvres, *tapas*. Most sell cigarettes and have a public telephone (the phrases you'll want are on pages 83 and 100). Here we tell you how to order your drinks: you normally pay for them when you leave rather than when they arrive.

un tinto *oon teen-tō*	a glass of red wine	**un blanco** *oon blang-kō*	a glass of white wine
una caña *oo-na kan-ya*	a glass of beer	**un coñac** *oon kon-yak*	a brandy
una ginebra *oo-na khee-nay-bra*	a gin	**un whisky** *oon wees-kee*	a whisky
un ron *oon ron*	a rum	**una vodka** *oo-na bod-ka*	a vodka

You may prefer a more typically Spanish apéritif:

un jerez *oon khe-reth*	sherry	**un vermut** *un ber-moot*	vermouth
un espumoso *oon es-poo-mō-sō*	sparkling wine	**un mosto** *oon mos-tō*	grape juice

and after dinner:

un anís *oon a-nees*	anise liqueur	**un sol y sombra** *oon sol ee som-bra*	brandy with anís

If you want a hot drink:

un café solo *oon ka-fay sō-lō*	black coffee	**un té con limón** *oon tay kon lee-mon*	lemon tea
un café con leche *oon ka-fay kon lay-chay*	coffee with milk	**un té con leche** *oon tay kon lay-chay*	tea with milk

Two chilled drinks are very common:

una horchata de almendra *oo-na or-cha-ta day al-men-dra*	a milky drink made from almonds	**un granizado de limón** *oon gra-nee-tha-dō day lee-mon*	a lemon drink with crushed ice

Eating & Drinking
Bars & Cafés

Other soft drinks for yourself or the children:

una gaseosa – lemonade
oon-na ga-say-ō-sa

una limonada – fizzy lemon drink
oo-na lee-mō-na-da

una naranjada – orangeade
oo-na na-rang-kha-da

un zumo de naranja – fresh orange juice
oon thoo-mō day na-rang-kha

un zumo de limón – fresh lemon juice
oon thoo-mō day lee-mon

If you're hungry you may be able to get some of these snacks.

un bocadillo . . . de jamón – a ham sandwich
oon bo-ka-deel-yō . . . day kha-mon

. . . de queso – a cheese sandwich
. . . day kay-sō

. . . de salchichón – a salami sandwich
day sal-chee-chon

un sandwich de jamón – a toasted ham sandwich
oon san-weech day kha-mon

patatas fritas – crisps (potato chips)
pa-ta-tas free-tas

un huevo duro – a hard-boiled egg
oon way-bō doo-rō

huevos con jamón – ham and eggs
way-bōs kon kha-mon

tortilla de patata – potato omelette
tor-teel-ya day pa-ta-ta

Wherever you go you can ask for *tapas* with your drinks.

aceitunas *a-the-ee-too-nas*	olives	**boquerones** *bo-kay-ro-nays*	anchovies
champiñones *cham-peen-yo-nays*	mushrooms	**gambas** *gam-bas*	prawns
calamares *ka-la-ma-rays*	squid	**mejillones** *me-kheel-yo-nays*	mussels

Paying

These phrases are needed in all sorts of places besides shops, so they have been collected together here.

How much is that?	– ¿Cuánto es eso? *kwan-tō es e-sō?*
I can't afford that much	– No puedo pagar tanto *no pway-dō pa-gar tan-tō*
What does that come to?	– ¿Cuánto hace eso? *kwan-tō a-thay e-sō?*
Are service and tax included?	– ¿Incluye servicio e impuestos? *een-kloo-yay ser-beeth-yō ay eem-pwes-tōs?*
How much is it ¿Cuánto cuesta *kwan-tō kwes-ta*	– **to get in?** la entrada? *la en-tra-da?*
	– **for a child?** para los niños? *pa-ra lōs neen-yōs?*
	– **to phone to Britain?** llamar por teléfono a Inglaterra? *lya-mar por tay-lay-fō-nō a* *eeng-gla-te-rra?*
How much is it ¿Cuánto es *kwan-tō es*	– **per person?** por persona? *por per-so-na?*
	– **per night?** por noche? *por no-chay?*
	– **per kilo?** por kilo? *por kee-lō?*
	– **per metre?** por metro? *por me-trō?*
	– **per kilometre?** por kilómetro? *por kee-lo-me-trō?*
Is there any extra charge?	– ¿Hay algún recargo? *a-ee al-goon ray-kar-gō?*

Paying

Is there a reduction for ¿Hay descuento para *a-ee des-**kwen**-tō pa-ra*	**– a group?** grupos? *groo-pōs?*
	– students? estudiantes? *es-tood-**yan**-tays?*
	– senior citizens? ancianos? *an-**thya**-nōs?*
Do I pay a deposit?	**–** ¿Tengo que pagar un depósito? ***teng**-gō kay pa-**gar** oon day-**po**-see-tō?*
Do I pay in advance or afterwards?	**–** ¿Le pago por adelantado o después? *lay-**pa**-gō por a-day-lan-**ta**-dō ō des-**pwes**?*
Do you accept traveller's cheques?	**–** ¿Aceptan cheques de viaje? *a-**thep**-tan **che**-kays day **bya**-khay?*
I want to pay by credit card	**–** Quería pagar con tarjeta de crédito *kay-**ree**-a pa-**gar** kon tar-**khay**-ta day **kre**-dee-tō*
Can I have an itemized bill?	**–** ¿Puede darme una factura detallada? ***pway**-day **dar**-may **oo**-na fak-**too**-ra day-tal-**ya**-da?*
Can I have a receipt?	**–** ¿Puede darme un recibo? ***pway**-day **dar**-may oon ray-**thee**-bō?*
I haven't enough money	**–** No tengo dinero suficiente *nō **teng**-gō dee-**nay**-rō soo-feeth-**yen**-tay*
You've given me the wrong change	**–** Me ha dado usted mal el cambio *may a **da**-dō oos-**ted** mal el **kamb**-yō*
Please forward it to this address	**–** Envíelo a esta dirección, por favor *en-**bee**-ay-lō a **es**-ta dee-rek-**thyon**, por fa-**bor***
Please pack it carefully	**–** Empaquételo con cuidado, por favor *em-pa-**kay**-tay-lō kon kwee-**da**-dō, por fa-**bor***

The Basic Phrases

I would like Quería *kay-**ree**-a*	**– a box of matches** una caja de cerillas *oo-na **ka**-kha day the-**reel**-yas*
	– some stamps sellos *sayl-yōs*
Do you sell sunglasses?	**–** ¿Venden gafas de sol? *ben-den **ga**-fas day sol?*
Have you got any ¿Tienen *tyay-nen*	**– English newspapers?** periódicos ingleses? *payr-yo-dee-kōs eeng-**glay**-says?*
	– toothpaste? pasta de dientes? ***pas**-ta day **dyen**-tays?*
I need some suntan oil	**–** Necesito aceite bronceador *nay-thay-**see**-tō a-**the**-ee-tay bron-thay-a-**dor***
Where is ¿Dónde está ***don**-day es-**ta***	**– the shoe department?** la sección de zapatos? *la sek-**thyon** day tha-**pa**-tōs?*
	– the food department? la sección de alimentación? *la sek-**thyon** day a-lee-men-tath-**yon**?*
Can I see ¿Puede enseñarme ***pway**-day en-sen-**yar**-may*	**– the hat in the window?** el sombrero del escaparate? *el som-**bray**-rō del es-ka-pa-**ra**-tay?*
	– that hat over there? aquel sombrero de allí? *a-**kel** som-**bray**-rō day al-**yee**?*
No, the other one	**–** No, el otro *nō, el **ō**-trō*
Have you got ¿Tiene *tyay-nay*	**– a larger one?** uno mayor? *oo-nō ma-**yor**?*
	– a smaller one? uno mas pequeno? *oo-nō mas pay-**kayn**-yō?*

The Basic Phrases

I'm just looking	– Sólo estoy mirando *sō-lō es-**toy** mee-**ran**-dō*
I'm looking for a blouse	– Estoy buscando una blusa *es-**toy** boos-**kan**-dō oo-na **bloo**-sa*
I like this one	– Me gusta ésta *may **goos**-ta **es**-ta*
I don't like it	– No me gusta *nō may **goos**-ta*
Have you got anything cheaper?	– ¿Tiene algo más barato? *tyay-nay **al**-gō mas ba-**ra**-tō?*
I'll take Me llevo *may **lyay**-bō*	– **this one** éste *es-tay*
	– **that one** ése *e-say*
	– **the other one** el otro *el **ō**-trō*
Please wrap it	– Envuélvamelo por favor *en-**bwel**-ba-may-lō por fa-**bor***
There's no need to wrap it	– No hace falta que lo envuelva *nō a-**thay** fal-ta kay lō en-**bwel**-ba*
Can I have a plastic bag?	– ¿Puede darme una bolsa de plástico? *pway-day **dar**-may oo-na **bol**-sa day **plas**-tee-kō?*

Food

Of course, you can solve all your language problems by heading for the nearest supermarket, but you will miss the personal touch of the shopkeepers and the people in the market.

I'd like — **a kilo of apples (2lb 3oz)**
Quería un kilo de manzanas
*kay-**ree**-a* *oon **kee**-lō day man-**tha**-nas*

— **a pound of tomatoes (1lb 1oz)**
medio de tomates
*may-dyō day tō-**ma**-tays*

— **250 grams of butter (9oz)**
un cuarto kilo de mantequilla
*oon **kwar**-tō **kee**-lō day man-tay-**keel**-ya*

— **100 grams of ground coffee**
cien gramos de café molido
*thyen **gra**-mōs day ka-**fay** mo-**lee**-dō*

— **5 slices of ham**
cinco lonchas de jamón
*theen-kō **lon**-chas day kha-**mon***

— **half a dozen eggs**
media docena de huevos
*may-dya do-**thay**-na day **way**-bōs*

A bag of sugar, please — Un paquete de azúcar, por favor
*oon pa-**kay**-tay day a-**thoo**-kar, por fa-bor*

A litre of milk, please — Un litro de leche, por favor
*oon **lee**-trō day **lay**-chay, por fa-**bor***

A bottle of wine, please — Una botella de vino
*oo-na bo-**tay**-lya day **bee**-nō*

2 pork chops, please — Dos chuletas de cerdo, por favor
*dōs choo-**lay**-tas day **ther**-dō, por fa-**bor***

A steak, please — Un filete, por favor
*oon fee-**lay**-tay, por fa-**bor***

Food
Meat & Fish

MEAT

beef	vaca *ba-ka*	**liver**	hígado *ee-ga-dō*
chicken	pollo *pol-yō*	**kidneys**	riñones *reen-yo-nays*
ham	jamón *kha-mon*	**pork**	cerdo *ther-dō*
lamb	cordero *kor-day-rō*	**veal**	ternera *ter-nay-ra*

FISH

baby eel	angula *ang-goo-la*	**red mullet**	salmonete *sal-mo-nay-tay*
clam	almeja *al-may-kha*	**salmon**	salmón *sal-mon*
cod	bacalao *ba-ka-la-ō*	**sardines**	sardinas *sar-dee-nas*
crab	cangrejo *kang-gray-khō*	**scallop**	vieira *bye-ee-ra*
crayfish	langostinos *lang-gos-tee-nōs*	**sea bream**	besugo *bay-soo-gō*
eel	anguila *ang-gee-la*	**sole**	lenguado *leng-gwa-dō*
hake	merluza *mer-loo-tha*	**sprat**	chanquete *chang-kay-tay*
herring	arenque *a-reng-kay*	**squid**	calamar *ka-la-mar*
John Dory	gallo *gal-yō*	**swordfish**	pez espada *peth es-pa-da*
lobster	langosta *lang-gos-ta*	**trout**	trucha *troo-cha*
oysters	ostras *os-tras*	**tuna**	atún *a-toon*
prawns	gambas *gam-bas*	**turbot**	rodaballo *ro-da-bal-yō*

Food
Groceries & Fruit

GROCERIES

baby food	comida para bebés *ko-**mee**-da **pa**-ra bay-bays*	**milk**	leche *lay-chay*
bread	pan *pan*	**oil**	aceite *a-**the**-ee-tay*
butter	mantequilla *man-tay-**keel**-ya*	**rice**	arroz *a-**rroth***
cheese	queso *kay-sō*	**salt**	sal *sal*
coffee	café *ka-fay*	**sugar**	azúcar *a-**thoo**-kar*
eggs	huevos *way-bōs*	**tea**	té *tay*
flour	harina *a-**ree**-na*	**vinegar**	vinagre *bee-**na**-gray*

FRUIT

apples	manzanas *man-**tha**-nas*	**oranges**	naranjas *na-**rang**-khas*
apricots	albaricoques *al-ba-ree-**ko**-kays*	**peach**	melocotón *me-lō-ko-**ton***
bananas	plátanos ***pla**-ta-nōs*	**pears**	peras *pay-ras*
cherries	cerezas *thay-**ray**-thas*	**pineapple**	piña *peen-ya*
grapefruit	pomelos *po-**may**-lōs*	**plums**	ciruelas *theer-**way**-las*
grapes	uvas *oo-bas*	**pomegranate**	granada *gra-**na**-da*
lemon	limón *lee-mon*	**raspberries**	frambuesas *fram-**bway**-sas*
melon	melón *me-lon*	**strawberries**	fresas *fray-sas*

Food
Vegetables & Herbs

artichoke	alcachofa *al-ka-chō-fa*	**leek**	puerro ***pway**-rrō*
asparagus	espárragos *es-**pa**-rra-gōs*	**lettuce**	lechuga *lay-**choo**-ga*
aubergine	berenjena *be-ren-**khay**-na*	**marrow**	calabacín *ka-la-ba-**theen***
avocado	aguacate *a-gwa-**ka**-tay*	**mint**	hierbabuena *yer-ba-**bway**-na*
broad beans	habas ***a**-bas*	**mushrooms**	champiñones *cham-peen-**yo**-nays*
Brussels sprouts	coles de Bruselas ***ko**-lays day broo-**say**-las*	**onions**	cebollas *thay-**bol**-yas*
cabbage	repollo *ray-**pol**-yō*	**parsley**	perejil *pay-ray-**kheel***
carrots	zanahoria *tha-na-**or**-ya*	**peas**	guisantes *gee-**san**-tays*
cauliflower	coliflor *ko-lee-**flor***	**potatoes**	patatas *pa-**ta**-tas*
celery	apio ***ap**-yō*	**radishes**	rábanos ***ra**-ba-nōs*
chicory	achicoria *a-chee-**hor**-ya*	**red pepper**	pimiento rojo *peem-**yen**-tō **rō**-khō*
chives	cebollinos *thay-bol-**yee**-nōs*	**sage**	salvia ***salb**-ya*
cucumber	pepino *pay-**pee**-nō*	**spinach**	espinaca *es-pee-**na**-ka*
eggplant	berenjena *be-ren-**khay**-na*	**squash**	calabacín *ka-la-ba-**theen***
French beans	judías verdes *khoo-**dee**-as **ber**-days*	**tomatoes**	tomates *tō-**ma**-tays*
garlic	ajo ***a**-khō*	**tarragon**	estragón *es-tra-**gon***
green pepper	pimiento verde *peem-**yen**-to **ber**-day*		

Newspapers & Stationery

If you want a newspaper, you'll get it at a news stand, *un quiosco de periódicos,* while stationery is generally sold along with books in a *librería-papelería.*

Have you got any
¿Tiene
tyay-nay

– **English newspapers?**
periódicos ingleses?
payr-yo-dee-kōs een-glay-says?

– **American newspapers?**
periódicos americanos?
payr-yo-dee-kōs a-may-ree-ka-nōs?

– **postcards?**
tarjetas postales?
tar-khay-tas pos-ta-lays?

I would like
Quería
kay-ree-a

– **some notepaper**
papel de escribir
pa-pel day es-kree-beer

– **some envelopes**
sobres
so-brays

– **a pen**
bolígrafo
bo-lee-gra-fō

– **a pencil**
un lápiz
oon la-peeth

I need
Necesito
nay-thay-see-tō

– **a bottle of ink**
un frasco de tinta
oon fras-kō day teen-ta

– **some adhesive tape**
cinta adhesiva
theen-ta a-day-see-ba

Do you sell
¿Venden
ben-den

– **English paperbacks?**
libros de bolsillo en inglés?
lee-brōs day bol-seel-yō en een-glays?

– **street maps?**
planos de la cuidad?
pla-nōs day la thyoo-dad?

Cigarettes

Tobacco is sold in little shops called *estancos*, which have a red, yellow and red sign outside saying *TABACALERA S.A.*, as well as in most bars and cafés. British and American brands are available along with the stronger Spanish ones. *Estancos* also sell stamps – you will find the phrases you want on page 99.

A packet of . . ., please –	Una cajetilla de . . ., por favor *oo-na ka-khay-**teel**-ya day . . ., por fa-**bor***
with filter-tip –	con filtro *kon **feel**-trō*
without filter –	sin filtro *seen **feel**-trō*
Have you got any American brands? –	¿Tiene alguna marca americana? *tyay-nay al-**goo**-na **mar**-ka a-may-ree-**ka**-na?*
Have you got any British brands? –	¿Tiene alguna marca inglesa? *tyay-nay al-**goo**-na **mar**-ka een-**glay**-sa?*
A pipe –	Una pipa *oo-na **pee**-pa*
A pouch of pipe tobacco –	Un paquete de tabaco de pipa *oon pa-**kay**-tay day ta-**ba**-kō day **pee**-pa*
Some pipe cleaners –	Escobillas (para limpiar pipas) *es-ko-**beel**-yas (**pa**-ra leem-**pyar pee**-pas)*
A box of matches –	Una caja de cerillas *oo-na **ka**-kha day the-**reel**-yas*
A cigar –	Un puro *oon **poo**-rō*
A cigarette lighter –	Un encendedor *oon en-then-day-**dor***
A gas (butane) refill –	Una carga para encendedor de gas *oo-na **kar**-ga **pa**-ra en-then-day-**dor** day gas*

The Chemist/Druggist

You should see the *If You're Ill* section if anybody's really unwell, but a chemist should be able to help you with the usual holiday ailments. There will be an illuminated green cross outside, and a sign saying *FARMACIA*. You won't find the range of toiletries and cosmetics sold in chemists at home, so for some of the items on the next page you will have to go to a *Perfumería* or a *Droguería*.

Can you give me something for a headache? – ¿Puede darme algo para el dolor de cabeza?
pway-day dar-may al-gō pa-ra el do-lor day ka-bay-tha?

I want something for insect bites – Quería algo para las picaduras de insectos
kay-ree-a al-gō pa-ra las pee-ka-doo-ras day een-sek-tōs

How many do I take? – ¿Cuántas tomo?
kwan-tas tō-mō?

How often do I take them? – ¿Cada cuánto las tomo?
ka-da kwan-tō las tō-mō?

Is this dangerous for children? – ¿Esto es peligroso para los niños?
es-tō es pay-lee-grō-sō pa-ra los neen-yōs?

You might also need something for:

chapped skin	piel agrietada *pyel a-gree-ay-ta-da*	**sunburn**	quemadura de sol *kay-ma-doo-ra day sol*
a cold	un resfriado *oon res-free-a-dō*	**toothache**	dolor de muelas *do-lor day mway-las*
hay fever	fiebre del heno *fee-ay-bray del ay-nō*	**travel sickness**	mareo *ma-ray-ō*
sore feet	pies cansados *pyays kan-sa-dōs*	**an upset stomach**	un transtorno estomacal *oon tras-tor-nō es-to-ma-kal*
sore throat	garganta irritada *gar-gan-ta ee-rree-ta-da*		

The Chemist/Druggist

aftershave	loción para después del afeitado *loth-yon pa-ra days-pwes del a-fe-ee-ta-dō*	**insect repellant**	loción contra insectos *lōth-yon kon-tra een-sek-tōs*
antihistamine	antihistamínico *an-tee-ees-ta-mee-nee-kō*	**kleenex**	pañuelos de papel *pany'-way-lōs day pa-pel*
antiseptic	antiséptico *an-tee-sep-tee-kō*	**laxative**	laxante *lak-san-tay*
aspirins	aspirinas *as-pee-ree-nas*	**lipstick**	lápiz de labios *la-peeth day la-byōs*
bandage	venda *ben-da*	**nail file**	lima *lee-ma*
band-aid	tiritas *tee-ree-tas*	**nail varnish**	esmalte de uñas *es-mal-tay day oon-yas*
blusher	colorete *ko-lo-ray-tay*	**nail varnish remover**	quitaesmalte *kee-ta-es-mal-tay*
cleansing milk	leche limpiadora *lay-chay leem-pya-dō-ra*	**perfume**	perfume *per-foo-may*
contraceptive	anticonceptivo *an-tee-kon-thep-tee-bō*	**powder**	polvos *pol-bōs*
cotton wool	algodón *al-go-don*	**razor blades**	cuchillas de afeitar *koo-cheel-yas day a-fe-ee-tar*
deodorant	desodorante *days-ō-dō-ran-tay*	**shampoo**	champú *cham-poo*
disinfectant	desinfectante *days een-fek-tan-tay*	**shaving cream**	crema de afeitar *kray-ma day a-fe-ee-tar*
eau de Cologne	agua de colonia *a-gwa day ko-lon-ya*	**skin moisturizer**	hidratante *ee-dra-tan-tay*
elastoplast	tiritas *tee-ree-tas*	**soap**	jabón *kha-bon*
eye shadow	sombra de ojos *som-bra day ō-khōs*	**suntan oil**	aceite bronceador *a-the-ee-tay bron-thay-a-dor*
hair spray	laca *la-ka*	**talc**	talco *tal-kō*
hand cream	crema de manos *kray-ma day ma-nōs*	**Tampax**	Tampax *tam-paks*
		toothpaste	pasta de dientes *pas-ta day dyen-tays*

Camera Shop

I need a film – **for this camera**
Necessito una película para esta cámara
*nay-thay-**see**-tō **oo**-na* *pa-ra es-ta **ka**-ma-ra*
*pay-**lee**-koo-la*

– **for this cine (movie) camera**
para este tomavistas
*pa-ra es-tay to-ma-**bees**-tas*

I want – **a black and white film**
Quiero una película en blanco y negro
kyay-rō *oo-na pay-**lee**-koo la en **blang**-kō ee*
nay-grō

– **a colour print film**
una película en color
*oo-na pay-**lee**-koo-la en ko-**lor***

– **a colour slide film**
una película de diapositivas en color
*oo-na pay-**lee**-la day dee-a-po-see-**tee**-bas*
*en ko-**lor***

– **some flash bulbs**
bombillas de flash
*bom-**beel**-yas day flash*

– **batteries for the flash**
pilas para el flash
*pee-las **pa**-ra el flash*

Can you develop this film – ¿Puede revelar esta película, por favor
please? *pway-day ray-bay-**lar** es-ta pay-**lee**-koo-la*
*por fa-**bor**?*

I would like 2 prints of this – Quería dos copias de esta
one *kay-**ree**-a dōs **kop**-yas day es-ta*

When will the photos be – ¿Para cuándo estarán las fotos?
ready? *pa-ra **kwan**-dō es-ta-ran las **fō**-tōs?*

I would like this photo – Quería una ampliación de esta foto
enlarged *kay-**ree**-a **oo**-na am-plee-ath-**yon** day es-ta*
fō-tō

There is something wrong – Mi cámara fotográfica no va bien
with my camera *mee **ka**-ma-ra fō-tō-**gra**-fee-ka nō ba byen*

The film is jammed – La película está atascada
*la pay-**lee**-koo-la es-**ta** a-tas-**ka**-da*

Camera Shop
Cameras & Accessories

accessory	accesorio *ak-thay-**so**-ryō*	**over exposed**	sobreexpuesto *sō-bray-eks-**pwes**-tō*
blue filter	filtro azul *feel-trō a-**thool***	**picture**	foto *fō-tō*
cassette	cassette *ka-**set***	**projector**	proyector *prō-yek-**tor***
cartridge	cartucho *kar-**too**-chō*	**print**	copia *kop-ya*
cine-camera	tomavistas *tō-ma-**bees**-tas*	**negative**	negativo *nay-ga-tee-bō*
distance	distancia *dees-**tan**-thya*	**red filter**	filtro rojo *feel-trō rō-khō*
enlargement	ampliación *am-plee-ath-**yon***	**reel**	carrete *ka-**rray**-tay*
exposure	exposición *eks-pō-seeth-**yon***	**rewind mechanism**	rebobinado *ray-bo-bee-**na**-dō*
exposure meter	fotómetro *fō-**to**-may-trō*	**shade**	parasol *pa-ra-**sol***
flash	flash *flash*	**slide**	diapositiva *dee-a-po-see-**tee**-ba*
flash bulb	bombilla de flash *bom-**beel**-ya day flash*	**shutter**	obturador *ob-too-ra-**dor***
flash cube	cubo de flash *koo-bō day flash*	**shutter speed**	velocidad de obturación *bay-lo-thee-**dad** day ob-too-rath-**yon***
focal distance	distancia focal *dees-**tanth**-ya fō-**kal***		
focus	enfoque *en-**fō**-kay*	**transparency**	diapositiva *dee-a-po-see-**tee**-ba*
in focus	enfocado *en-fō-**ka**-dō*	**tripod**	trípode *tree-po-day*
out of focus	desenfocado *days-en-fō-**ka**-dō*	**under- exposed**	subexpuesto *soob-eks-**pwes**-tō*
image	imagen *ee-**ma**-khen*	**viewfinder**	visor *bee-**sor***
lens	lente *len-tay*	**wide-angle lens**	lente granangular *len-tay gran-ang-goo-**lar***
lens cover	tapa de lente *ta-pa day len-tay*		
movie camera	tomavistas *tō-ma-**bees**-tas*	**yellow filter**	filtro amarillo *feel-trō a-ma-**reel**-yō*

Clothes
Sizes

First of all you'll want some idea of your continental size. Unfortunately slight variations in sizes mean that these can only be approximate equivalents.

Dresses

UK	10	12	14	16	18
US	8	10	12	14	16
Spain	36	38	40	42	44

Ladies' sweaters

UK/US	32	34	36	38	40
Spain	36	38	40	42	44

Ladies' shoes

UK	3	3½	4	4½	5	5½	6	6½
US	4½	5	5½	6	6½	7	7½	8
Spain	35	36	37	37½	38	38½	39	40

Men's shoes

UK	7	8	9	10	11
US	8½	9½	10½	11½	12½
Spain	40½	42	43	44	45½

Clothes Sizes

Men's suits

UK/US	36	38	40	42	44	46
Spain	46	48	50	52	54	56

Waist and chest measurements

inches	28	30	32	34	36	38	40
centimetres	71	76	81	87	91	97	102

inches	42	44	46	48	50	52	54
centimetres	107	112	117	122	127	132	138

Men's shirts

UK/US	14	14½	15	15½	16	16½	17
Spain	36	37	38	39	41	42	43

Clothes

I would like	– **a dress**
Quería	un vestido
*kay-**ree**-a*	*oon bes-**tee**-dō*
	– **a sweater**
	un jersey
	*oon **kher**-se-ee*
I take a continental size 40	– Uso la talla cuarenta
	*oo-sō la **tal**-ya kwa-**ren**-ta*
I take a continental shoe size 40	– Calzo un cuarenta
	***kal**-thō oon kwa-**ren**-ta*
Can you measure me?	– ¿Puede medirme?
	***pway**-day may-**deer**-may?*
Have you got something in blue?	– ¿Tiene algo en azul?
	***tyay**-nay **al**-gō en a-**thool**?*
What is the material?	– ¿Qué tela es?
	*kay **tay**-la es?*
I like	– **this one**
Me gusta	éste
*may **goos**-ta*	***es**-tay*
	– **that one there**
	aquél de allí
	*a-**kel** day al-**yee***
	– **the one in the window**
	el del escaparate
	*el del es-ka-pa-**ra**-tay*
May I take it over to the light?	– ¿Puedo llevarlo a la luz?
	***pway**-dō lyay-**bar**-lō a la looth?*
May I try it on?	– ¿Puedo probarlo?
	***pway**-dō prō-**bar**-lō?*
Where are the changing (dressing) rooms?	– ¿Donde están los probadores?
	***don**-day es-**tan** lōs prō-ba-**do**-rays?*
I want a mirror	– ¿Un espejo, por favor?
	*oon es-**pay**-khō, por fa-**bor**?*
I like it	– Me gusta
	*may **goos**-ta*

Clothes

I don't like it	– No me gusta *nō may **goos**-ta*
It doesn't fit properly	– No sienta bien *nō **syen**-ta byen*
It doesn't suit me	– No me va bien *nō may ba byen*
I want Quiero ***kyay**-rō*	– **a bigger one** uno mayor *oo-nō ma-**yor***
	– **a smaller one** uno más pequeño *oo-nō mas pay-**kayn**-yō*
	– **one without a belt** uno sin cinturón *oo-nō seen theen-too-**ron***
Is this all you have?	– ¿No tienen más que ésto? *nō **tyay**-nen mas kay **es**-tō?*
I'll take it	– Me lo llevo *may lō **lyay**-bō*
Is it washable?	– ¿Es lavable? *es la-**ba**-blay?*
Will it shrink?	– ¿Encogerá? *en-ko-khay-**ra**?*
Must it be dry-cleaned?	– ¿Hay que limpiarlo en seco? *a-ee kay leem-**pyar**-lō en **say**-kō?*

Clothes

blouse	blusa *bloo-sa*	**shorts**	pantalón corto *pan-ta-lon kor-tō*
bra	sujetador *soo-khay-ta-dor*	**skirt**	falda *fal-da*
cardigan	chaqueta de punto *cha-kay-ta day poon-tō*	**slip**	combinación *kom-bee-nath-yon*
coat	abrigo *a-bree-gō*	**sneakers**	zapatillas de deporte *tha-pa-teel-yas day day-por-tay*
dress	vestido *bes-tee-dō*	**socks**	calcetines *kal-thay-tee-nays*
dungarees	mono *mō-nō*	**stockings**	medias *med-yas*
gloves	guantes *gwan-tays*	**suit (man's)**	traje (de caballero) *tra-khay (day ka-bal-yay-rō)*
hat	sombrero *som-bray-rō*	**suit (woman's)**	traje (de señora) *tra-khay (day sayn-yō-ra)*
jacket	chaqueta *cha-kay-ta*	**sweater**	jersey *kher-se-ee*
jeans	vaqueros *ba-kay-rōs*		
nightdress	camisón *ka-mee-son*	**swimming costume**	traje de baño *tra-khay day ban-yō*
panties	braga *bra-ga*	**tie**	corbata *kor-ba-ta*
petticoat	combinación *kom-bee-na-thyon*	**tights**	pantys *pan-tees*
pullover	jersey *kher-see-ee*	**towel**	toalla *tō-al-ya*
pyjamas	pijama *pee-kha-ma*	**trousers**	pantalones *pan-ta-lo-nays*
raincoat	impermeable *eem-per-may-a-blay*	**T shirt**	camiseta *ka-mee-say-ta*
sandals	sandalias *san-dal-yas*	**underpants**	calzoncillos *kal-thon-theel-yōs*
scarf	pañuelo *pany'-way-lō*	**vest**	camiseta *ka-mee-say-ta*
shirt	camisa *ka-mee-sa*		

MATERIALS

acrylic	acrílico
	*a-**kree**-lee-kō*
corduroy	pana
	***pa**-na*
cotton	algodón
	*al-go-**don***
denim	vaquero
	*ba-**kay**-rō*
fur	pieles
	***pyel**-ays*
jersey	jersey
	***kher**-se-ee*
lace	encaje
	*en-**ka**-khay*
leather	piel
	pyel
linen	hilo
	***ee**-lō*
nylon	nylón
	*nee-**lon***
polyester	polyester
	*po-lee-**es**-ter*
poplin	popelín
	*po-pay-**leen***
rayon	rayón
	*ra-**yon***
silk	seda
	***say**-da*
suede	ante
	***an**-tay*
terylene	terylene
	*tay-ree-**leen***
velvet	terciopelo
	*terth-yō-**pay**-lō*
wash and wear	lavar y poner
	*la-**bar** ee po-**ner***
wool	lana
	***la**-na*

ACCESSORIES

belt	cinturón
	*theen-too-**ron***
bracelet	pulsera
	*pool-**say**-ra*
brooch	broche
	***bro**-chay*
button	botón
	*bo-**ton***
earrings	pendientes
	*pend-**yen**-tays*
handbag	bolso
	***bol**-sō*
handkerchief	pañuelo
	*pany'-**way**-lō*
necklace	collar
	*kol-**yar***
pendant	colgante
	*kol-**gan**-tay*
purse	(UK) monedero
	*mo-nay-**day**-rō*
	(US) bolso
	***bol**-so*
ring	anillo
	*a-**neel**-yō*
umbrella	paraguas
	*pa-**ra**-gwas*
wallet	cartera
	*kar-**tay**-ra*
watch	reloj
	*ray-**lokh***
zip	cierre relámpago
	***thay**-rray ray-**lam**-pa-gō*

The Hairdresser

I'd like to make an appointment	– Quería pedir hora *kay-**ree**-a pay-**deer** ō-ra*
I want Quiero ***kyay**-rō*	– **a cut** cortar *kor-**tar***
	– **a razor cut** un corta navaja *oon **kor**-tay na-**ba**-kha*
	– **a trim** cortar las puntas *kor-**tar** las **poon**-tas*
I want my hair Quiero el pelo ***kyay**-rō el **pay**-lō*	– **fairly short** bastante corto *bas-**tan**-tay **kor**-tō*
	– **not too short** no muy corto *nō mwee **kor**-tō*
	– **short and curly** corto y rizado ***kor**-tō ee ree-**tha**-dō*
	– **layered** en capas *en **ka**-pas*
	– **in a fringe** con flequillo *kon flay-**keel**-yō*
Take more off Córteme más ***kor**-tay-may mas*	– **the front** por delante *por day-**lan**-tay*
	– **the back** por detrás *por day-**tras***
Not too much off No me corte mucho *nō may **kor**-tay **moo**-chō*	– **the sides** a los lados ⌐ *a lōs **la**-dōs*
	– **the top** por arriba *por a-**rree**-ba*

The Hairdresser

I'd like	**– a perm (permanent)**
Quería	una permanente
kay-**ree**-a	**oo**-na per-ma-**nen**-tay
	– a light perm
	una permanente suave
	oo-na per-ma-**nen**-tay **swa**-bay
	– a shampoo and set
	lavar y marcar
	la-**bar** ee mar-**kar**
	– a blow-dry
	un moldeado con secador de mano
	oon mol-day-**a**-dō kon say-ka-**dor** day
	ma-nō
	– my hair tinted
	teñir el pelo
	tayn-**yeer** el **pay**-lō
	– my hair streaked
	ponerme vetas
	po-**ner**-may **bay**-tas
The water is too hot	**–** El agua está demasiado caliente
	el **ag**-wa es-ta day-mas-**ya**-dō kal-**yen**-tay
The dryer is too hot	**–** El secador está demasiado caliente
	el say-ka-**dor** es-**ta** day-mas-**ya**-dō
	kal-**yen**-tay
I'd like	**– a conditioner**
Quería	un acondicionador
kay-**ree**-a	oon a-kon-deeth-yo-na-**dor**
	– hair spray
	laca
	la-ka
That's fine, thank you	**–** Así está bien, gracias
	a-**see** es-**ta** byen, **grath**-yas

Dry Cleaners & Laundry

A dry-cleaner's is called *una tintorería* or *un limpieza en seco*; sometimes it is combined with *una lavandería* or laundry which will usually provide a fairly quick service. If you don't mind the chore of doing it yourself, you should look for *una lavandería automática*.

Will you	– **clean this skirt?**
¿Puede	limpiar esta falda?
pway-day	*leem-pyar es-ta fal-da?*
	– **press these trousers?**
	planchar estos pantalones?
	plan-char es-tōs pan-ta-lo-nays?
	– **wash and iron these shirts?**
	lavar y planchar estas camisas?
	la-bar ee plan-char es-tas ka-mee-sas?
	– **wash these clothes?**
	lavar esta ropa?
	la-bar es-ta rō-pa?
This stain is	– **grease**
Esta mancha es de	grasa
es-ta man-cha es day	*gra-sa*
	– **ink**
	tinta
	teen-ta
	– **blood**
	sangre
	sang-gray
	– **coffee**
	café
	ka-fay
This fabric is delicate	– Este tejido es delicado
	es-tay tay-khee-dō es day-lee-ka-dō
Can you sew these buttons on please?	– ¿Puede coser estos botones, por favor?
	pway-day ko-ser es-tōs bo-to-nays, por fa-bor?
When will my things be ready?	– ¿Para cuándo estarán mis cosas?
	pa-ra kwan-dō es-ta-ran mees kō-sas?
I need them in a hurry	– Lo necesito urgentemente
	lō nay-thay-see-tō oor-khen-tay-men-tay

There is something wrong – Mi cámara fotográfica no va bien
with my camera   *mee ka-ma-ra fō-tō-gra-fee-ka nō ba byen*

This is – **broken**
Esto está   roto
es-tō es-ta   *rō-tō*

     – **damaged**
     estropeado
     es-trō-pay-a-dō

     – **torn**
     rasgado
     ras-ga-dō

Would you have a look at – Puede echarle una ojeada a esto, por
this, please?   favor?
   pway-day ay-char-lay oo-na o-khay-a-da
   a es-tō por fa-bor?

Can you fix it? – ¿Puede arreglarlo?
   pway-day a-rray-glar-lō?

Can you reheel these shoes? – Puede ponerme tapas a estos zapatos?
   pway-day po-ner-may ta-pas a es-tōs
   tha-pa-tōs?

Have you got a replacement – ¿Tiene un repuesto?
part?   *tyay-nay oon ray-pwes-tō?*

When will it be ready? – ¿Para cuándo estará?
   pa-ra kwan-dō es-ta-ra?

Can you do it quickly? – ¿Puede hacérmelo rápido?
   pway-day a-ther-may-lō ra-pee-dō?

Can you give me – **some strong glue?**
¿Puede darme   pegamento fuerte?
pway-day dar-may   *pay-ga-men-tō fwer-tay?*

     – **some string?**
     una cuerda?
     oo-na kwer-da?

     – **a needle and thread?**
     aguja e hilo?
     a-goo-kha ay ee-lō?

The Bank

Banks are usually open from 9 a.m. until 2 p.m., including Saturdays.

Will you change – **these travellers' cheques?**
¿Pueden cambiarme estos cheques de viaje?
pway-den kam-byar-may *es-tōs che-kays day bya-khay?*

– **these notes (bills)?**
estos billetes?
es-tōs beel-yay-tays?

What is the rate for – **sterling?**
¿A cómo está la libra esterlina?
a kō-mō es-ta *la lee-bra es-ter-lee-na?*

– **dollars?**
el dólar?
el do-lar?

Here is my passport – Aquí está mi pasaporte
a-kee es-ta mee pa-sa-por-tay

I would like to cash a cheque – Quería hacer efectivo un cheque con la
with my Eurocheque card tarjeta de eurocheque
kay-ree-a a-ther ay-fek-tee-bō oon che-kay kon la tar-khay-ta day e-oo-rō-che-kay

I would like to obtain a cash – Quería obtener dinero en efectivo con
advance with my credit card mi tarjeta de crédito
kay-ree-a ob-te-ner dee-nay-rō en ay-fek-tee-bō kon mee tar-khay-ta day kre-dee-tō

What is your commission? – ¿Qué comisión cobran ustedes?
kay ko-mees-yon ko-bran oos-tay-days?

Can you contact my bank to – ¿Pueden ponerse en contacto con mi
arrange for a transfer please? banco para pedir una transferencia, por favor?
pway-den po-ner-say en kon-tak-tō kon mee bang-kō pa-ra a-ther oo-na trans-fe-renth-ya, por fabor?

This is the name and address – Este es el nombre y la dirección de mi
of my bank banco
es-tay es el nom-bray ee la dee-rek-thyon day mee bang-kō

The Post Office

A large Spanish post office can be rather confusing with a long row of desks, each providing a specific service. The ones you are most likely to need are those dealing with stamps – *venta de sellos* – and parcels – *paquetes*. If you just want stamps it's simpler to get them from an *estanco*.

How much is a letter	**– to Britain?**
¿Qué franqueo lleva una carta	a Inglaterra?
kay fran-kay-ō lyay-ba oo-na	*a eeng-gla-te-rra?*
kar-ta	
	– to the United States?
	a los Estados Unidos?
	a lōs es-ta-dōs oo-nee-dōs?
Six 25 peseta stamps, please	– Seis sellos de veinticinco pesetas, por favor
	se-ees sel-yōs day be-een-tay-theeng-kō pay-say-tas, por fa-bor
Can I have 6 stamps for postcards to Britain?	– ¿Me da seis sellos para tarjetas postales a Inglatera?
	may da se-ees sel-yōs pa-ra tar-khay-tas pos-ta-lays a eeng-gla-te-rra?
I want to send this parcel	– Quiero enviar este paquete
	kway-rō en-byar es-tay pa-kay-tay
I want to send a telegram	– Quiero poner un telegrama
	kyay-rō po-ner oon tay-lay-gra-ma
Can I have a telegram form please?	– ¿Me da un impreso para telegrama, por favor?
	may da oon eem-pray-sō pa-ra tay-lay-gra-ma, por fa-bor?
When will it arrive?	– ¿Cuándo llegará?
	kwan-dō lyay-ga-ra?
I want to send this by registered post	– Quiero enviar esto por correo certificado
	kyay-rō en-byar es-tō por ko-rray-ō ther-tee-fee-ka-dō

Using the Telephone

The simplest, but most expensive way to telephone is from your hotel. Otherwise, you can go to a *central telefónica*. Tell the clerk the country or place you want and she will direct you to a box. You dial the number yourself and the clerk will charge you afterwards, but she will connect you for person-to-person and reverse charge (collect) calls. Pay phones in the street and in bars require coins, but in some bars you pay after the call and sometimes you still need telephone tokens or *fichas*.

I would like to make a phone call to Britain –
Quería hacer una llamada telefónica a Inglaterra
*kay-**ree**-a a-**ther** oo-na lya-ma-da tay-lay-fo-nee-ka a eeng-gla-**te**-rra*

Can you get me this number? –
¿Puede usted obtenerme esto número?
***pway**-day oos-**ted** ob-te-**ner**-may es-tay **noo**-may-rō?*

I wish to make a reversed charge (collect) call –
Quiero hacer una llamada a cobro revertido
*kyay-rō a-**ther** oo-na lya-**ma**-da a **ko**-brō ray-ber-**tee**-dō*

I wish to make a person-to-person call to Señora Carrera –
Quiero poner una conferencia personal con la Señora Carrera
*kyay-rō po-**ner** oo-na kon-fay-**renth**-ya per-so-**nal** kon la sayn-**yor**-a ka-**rray**-ra*

Which box do I use? –
¿Qué cabina uso?
*kay ka-**bee**-na oo-sō?*

May I use the telephone please? –
¿Puedo usar el teléfono, por favor?
***pway**-dō oo-**sar** el tay-**lay**-fo-nō, por fa-**bor**?*

Do I need a token? –
¿Hace falta ficha?
*a-thay **fal**-ta **fee**-cha?*

Can I speak to Señora Carrera? –
¿Podría hablar con la señora Carrera´
*po-**dree**-a a-**blar** kon la sayn-**yor**-a ka-**rray**-ra?*

I have a crossed line –
Hay un cruce de línea
*a-ee oon **kroo**-thay day **lee**-nay-a*

Using the Telephone

We have been cut off – Se ha cortado la comunicación
*say a kor-**ta**-dō la kō-moo-nee-kath-**yon***

You may hear somebody at the other end of the line say:

Diga
dee-ga
Dígame
dee-ga-may
– Hello

Le paso con la Señora Carrera – I'm putting you through to Señora Carrera
*lay **pa**-sō kon la sayn-**yo**-ra ka-**rray**-ra*

No cuelgue
*no **kwel**-gay*
Un momento, por favor
*oon mo-**men**-tō, por fa-**bor***
– Hold the line

Estoy intentando ponerle – I'm trying to connect you
*es-**toy** een-ten-tan-**dō** po-**ner**-lay*

Está comunicando – The line is engaged (busy)
*es-**ta** ko-moo-nee-**kan**-dō*

Ese número está estropeado – This number is out of order
*e-say **noo**-may-rō es-**ta** es-trō-pay-**a**-dō*

Ese número no puede obternerlo desde ese teléfono – This number cannot be obtained from this telephone
*e-say **noo**-may-rō nō **pway**-day ob-te-**ner**-lō des-day e-say tay-**lay**-fo-nō*

No puedo conseguirle la comunicación – I cannot obtain this number
*no **pway**-dō kon-say-**geer**-lay la ko-moo-nee-ka-**thyon***

Hable, por favor – Please go ahead
*a-blay, por fa-**bor***

Señora Carrera al habla – Señora Carrera speaking
*sayn-**yo**-ra ka-**rray**-ra al **a**-bla*

Accidents

If a visit to a doctor is necessary, you will probably have to pay on the spot, so make sure you are properly insured before you leave. Normal body temperature on a Centigrade thermometer is 37°, so a reading of 38° means a temperature of 100°.

There has been an accident	– Ha habido un accidente *a a-**bee**-dō oon ak-thee-**den**-tay*
Call an ambulance	– Llame a una ambulancia ***lya**-may a **oo**-na am-boo-**lanth**-ya*
Get a doctor	– Traiga a un médico ***tra**-ee-ga a oon **me**-dee-kō*
He is unconscious	– Ha perdido el conocimiento *a per-**dee**-dō el ko-no-thee-**myen**-tō*
She has been seriously injured	– Está gravemente herida *es-**ta** gra-ba-**men**-tay ay-**ree**-da*
He has been badly hurt	– Tiene una herida seria ***tyay**-nay **oo**-na ay-**ree**-da **ser**-ya*
Can I have an appointment with the doctor?	– Quería solicitar una cita con el doctor *kay-**ree**-a so-lee-thee-**tar oo**-na **thee**-ta kon el dok-**tor***
I have cut myself	– Me he cortado *may ay kor-**ta**-dō*
He has burnt himself	– Se ha quemado *say a kay-**ma**-dō*
She has a temperature	– Tiene fiebre ***tyay**-nay **fyay**-bray*
I have hurt Me he hecho daño *may ay **ay**-chō **dan**-yō*	– **my arm** en el brazo *en el **bra**-thō*
	– **my leg** en la pierna *en la **pyer**-na*
I have a pain here	– Tengo un dolor aquí ***teng**-gō oon do-**lor** a-**kee***
I have had a fall	– Me he caído *may ay ka-**ee**-dō*

Accidents

He has been stung	– Tiene una picadura *tyay-nay **oo**-na pee-ka-**doo**-ra*
She has been bitten by a dog	– La ha mordido un perro *la a mor-**dee**-dō oon pe-rrō*
I have broken my arm	– Me he roto el brazo *may ay **rō**-tō el **bra**-thō*
He has dislocated his shoulder	– Se ha dislocado el hombro *say a dees-lō-**ka**-dō el om-brō*
She has sprained Se ha torcido *say a tor-**thee**-dō*	– **her ankle** el tobillo *el to-**beel**-yō*
	– **her wrist** la muñeca *la moon-**yay**-ka*
I have pulled a muscle	– Me he dado un tirón en un músculo *may ay **da**-dō oon tee-**ron** en oon **moos**-koo-lō*
There is a swelling here	– Tengo esto hinchado ***teng**-gō **es**-tō een-**cha**-dō*
It is inflamed here	– Está inflamado aquí *es-**ta** een-fla-ma-dō a-**kee***
It is painful Me duele *may **dway**-lay*	– **to walk** al andar *al an-**dar***
	– **to swallow** al tragar *al tra-**gar***
	– **to breathe** al respirar *al res-pee-**rar***
I have cramp	– Tengo un calambre ***teng**-gō oon ka-**lam**-bray*
I have a rash here	– Tengo una erupción aquí ***teng**-gō **oo**-na ay-roop-**thyon** a-**kee***

Symptoms

I cannot sleep –	No puedo dormir *nō* **pway**-*dō dor-***meer**
I have – Tengo *teng-***gō**	**a headache** dolor de cabeza *do-***lor** *day ka-***bay**-*tha*
–	**an earache** dolor de oídos *do-***lor** *day o-ee-***dōs**
–	**a sore throat** irritación de garganta *ee-rree-tath-***yon** *day gar-***gan**-*ta*
I have sunstroke –	Tengo insolación *teng-***gō** *een-sō-lath-***yon**
My tongue is coated –	Tengo la lengua cargada *teng-***gō** *la* **leng**-*gwa kar-***ga**-*da*
My stomach is upset –	Me duele el estómago *may* **dway**-*lay el es-***to**-*ma-***gō**
I feel nauseous (nauseated) –	Siento náuseas *syen-***tō** *na-oo-say-as*
I think I have food poisoning –	Creo que tengo intoxicación por alimentos **kray**-*ō kay* **teng**-*gō een-tok-see-kath-***yon** *por a-lee-***men**-*tōs*
I have been sick –	He vomitado *ay bo-mee-***ta**-*dō*
I have diarrhoea –	Tengo diarrea *teng-***gō** *dee-a-***rray**-*a*
I am constipated –	Tengo estreñimiento *teng-***gō** *es-trayn-yeem-***yen**-*tō*
I feel faint –	Me siento débil *may* **syen**-*tō* **de**-*beel*
I am allergic to penicillin –	Soy alérgico a la penicilina *soy a-***ler**-*khee-kō a la pay-nee-thee-***lee**-*na*
I have high blood pressure –	Tengo la tensión alta *teng-***gō** *la ten-***syon** **al**-*ta*

Conditions

I am a diabetic –	Soy diabético *soy dya-**bay**-tee-kō*
I am taking these drugs –	Estoy tomando estos medicamentos *es-**toy** tō-**man**-dō es-tōs* *may-dee-ka-**men**-tōs*
Can you give me a Spanish prescription for them? –	¿Puede darme una receta española para esto? *pway-day **dar**-may oo-na ray-**thay**-ta* *es-pan-**yo**-la **pa**-ra es-**tō**?*
I am pregnant –	Estoy embarazada *es-**toy** em-ba-ra-**tha**-da*
I am on the pill –	Estoy tomando la píldora *es-**toy** tō-**man**-dō la **peel**-do-ra*
My blood group is . . . –	Mi grupo sanguíneo es . . . *mee **groo**-pō sang-**gee**-nay-ō es*
I don't know my blood group –	No sé mi grupo sanguíneo *no say mee **groo**-pō sang-**gee**-nay-ō*
Must I stay in bed? –	¿Tengo que quedarme en la cama? ***teng**-gō kay kay-**dar**-may en la **ka**-ma?*
How soon can I travel? –	¿Cuando podré viajar? ***kwan**-dō po-**dray** bya-**khar**?*
Will I be able to go out tomorrow? –	¿Podré salir mañana? *po-**dray** sa-**leer** man-ya-na?*
Will I have to go into hospital? –	¿Tendré que ir al hospital? *ten-**dray** kay eer al os-pee-**tal**?*
Will an operation be necessary? –	¿Hará falta operar? *a-**ra** fal-ta o-pay-**rar**?*

Parts of the body

adenoids	adenoides *a-day-noy-days*	**kidney**	riñón *reen-yon*
ankle	tobillo *tō-beel-yō*	**knee**	rodilla *ro-deel-ya*
arm	brazo *bra-thō*	**leg**	pierna *pyer-na*
back	espalda *es-pal-da*	**liver**	hígado *ee-ga-dō*
bone	hueso *way-sō*	**lungs**	pulmones *pool-mo-nays*
breast	pecho *pay-chō*	**mouth**	boca *bo-ka*
cheek	mejilla *may-kheel-ya*	**muscle**	músculo *moos-koo-lō*
chest	pecho *pay-chō*	**neck**	cuello *kwel-yō*
chin	barbilla *bar-beel-ya*	**nose**	nariz *na-reeth*
ear	oreja *o-ray-kha*	**shin**	espinilla *es-pee-neel-ya*
elbow	codo *kō-dō*	**skin**	piel *pyel*
eye	ojo *ō-khō*	**skull**	cráneo *kra-nay-ō*
face	cara *ka-ra*	**spine**	columna vertebral *ko-loom-na ber-tay-bral*
finger	dedo *day-dō*		
foot	pie *pyay*	**stomach**	estómago *es-to-ma-gō*
forearm	antebrazo *an-tay-bra-thō*	**toe**	dedo del pie *day-dō del pyay*
forehead	frente *fren-tay*	**thigh**	muslo *moos-lō*
hand	mano *ma-nō*	**throat**	garganta *gar-gan-ta*
heart	corazón *ko-ra-thon*	**thumb**	pulgar *pool-gar*
heel	talón *ta-lon*	**tonsils**	anginas *ang-khee-nas*
		wrist	muñeca *moon-yay-ka*

Dentist

I need to see the dentist –	Necesito ver al dentista *nay-thay-**see**-tō ber al den-**tees**-ta*
I have a toothache –	Me duele una muela *may **dway**-lay **oo**-na **mway**-la*
It's this one –	Es ésta *es **es**-ta*
I've broken a tooth –	Me he roto un diente *may ay **rō**-tō oon **dyen**-tay*
The filling has come out –	Se me ha caído el empaste *say may a ka-**ee**-dō el em-**pas**-tay*
Will you have to take it out? –	¿Tendré que sacarla? *ten-**dray** kay sa-**kar**-la?*
Are you going to fill it? –	¿Va a empastarla? *ba a em-pas-**tar**-la?*
That hurt –	Eso dolió mucho *e-sō dol-**yō** moo-chō*
Please give me an injection –	Póngame una inyección, por favor ***pong**-ga-may **oo**-na een-yek-**thyon**, por fa-**bor***
My gums hurt –	Me duelen las encías *may **dway**-len las en-**thee**-as*
My false teeth are broken –	Se me ha roto la dentadura postiza *say may a **rō**-tō la den-ta-**doo**-ra pos-**tee**-tha*
Can you repair them? –	¿Puede arreglarla? ***pway**-day a-rray-**glar**-la?*

The Time

What time is it?	–	¿Qué hora es? *kay ō-ra es?*
It is ...	–	Son ... *son ...*
10 o'clock	–	las diez *las dyeth*
5 past 10	–	las diez y cinco *las dyeth ee theeng-kō*
10 past 10	–	las diez y diez *las dyeth ee dyeth*
a quarter past 10	–	las diez y cuarto *las dyeth ee kwar-tō*
20 past 10	–	las diez y veinte *las dyeth ee be-een-tay*
25 past 10	–	las diez y veinticinco *las dyeth ee be-een-tee-theeng-kō*
half past 10	–	las diez y media *las dyeth ee me-dya*
25 to 11	–	las once menos veinticinco *las on-thay may-nōs be-een-tee-theeng-kō*
20 to 11	–	las once menos veinte *las on-thay may-nōs be-een-tay*
a quarter to 11	–	las once menos cuarto *las on-thay may-nōs kwar-tō*
10 to 11	–	las once menos diez *las on-thay may-nōs dyeth*
5 to 11	–	las once menos cinco *las on-thay may-nōs theeng-kō*
11 o'clock	–	las once *las on-thay*
12 o'clock (midday)	–	las doce (mediodía) *las do-thay (may-dyō-dee-a)*
(midnight)	–	las doce (medianoche) *las do-thay (may-dya-no-chay)*

The Time

A few of these expressions may be useful.

tonight	–	esta noche *es-ta no-chay*
at night	–	por la noche *por la no-chay*
the morning	–	la mañana *la man-ya-na*
this afternoon	–	esta tarde *es-ta tar-day*
before midnight	–	antes de medianoche *an-tays day may-dya-no-chay*
after 3 o'clock	–	después de las tres *des-pways day las tres*
at half past 6	–	a las seis y media *a las se-ees ee may-dya*
nearly 5 o'clock	–	casi las cinco *ka-see las theeng-kō*
at about 1 o'clock	–	hacia la una *ath-ya la oo-na*
in an hour's time	–	dentro de una hora *den-trō day oo-na o-ra*
two hours ago	–	hace dos horas *a-thay dōs ō-ras*
in half an hour	–	dentro de media hora *den-trō day may-dya ō-ra*
soon	–	pronto *pron-tō*
early	–	temprano *tem-pra-nō*
late	–	tarde *tar-day*

Numbers
Up to a Million

0	cero	20	veinte
	thay-rō		*be-een-tay*
1	uno	21	veintiuno
	oo-nō		*be-een-tee-oo-nō*
2	dos	22	veintidós
	dōs		*be-een-tee-dōs*
3	tres	23	veintitrés
	tres		*be-een-tee-tres*
4	cuatro	30	treinta
	kwa-trō		*tre-een-ta*
5	cinco	40	cuarenta
	theeng-kō		*kwa-ren-ta*
6	seis	50	cincuenta
	se-ees		*theeng-kwen-ta*
7	siete	60	sesenta
	syay-tay		*se-sen-ta*
8	ocho	70	setenta
	o-chō		*se-ten-ta*
9	nueve	80	ochenta
	nway-bay		*o-chen-ta*
10	diez	90	noventa
	dyeth		*no-ben-ta*
11	once	100	cien
	on-thay		*thyen*
12	doce	110	ciento diez
	do-thay		*thyen-tō dyeth*
13	trece	200	doscientos
	tre-thay		*dos-thyen-tōs*
14	catorce	300	trescientos
	ka-tor-thay		*tres-thyen-tōs*
15	quince	400	cuatrocientos
	keen-thay		*kwat-rō-thyen-tōs*
16	dieciséis	500	quinientos
	dye-thee-se-ees		*keen-yen-tōs*
17	diecisiete	1,000	mil
	dye-thee-syay-tay		*meel*
18	dieciocho	2,000	dos mil
	dye-thee-o-chō		*dōs meel*
19	diecinueve	1,000,000	un millón
	dye-thee-nway-bay		*oon meel-yon*

Numbers
The First to the Last

1st	primero *pree-**may**-rō*	16th	decimosexto *de-thee-mō-**seks**-tō*
2nd	segundo *say-**goon**-dō*	17th	decimoséptimo *de-thee-mō-**sep**-tee- mō*
3rd	tercero *ter-**thay**-rō*	18th	decimoctavo *de-thee-mō-ok-**ta**-bō*
4th	cuarto ***kwar**-tō*	19th	decimonoveno *de-thee-mō-nō-**bay**-nō*
5th	quinto ***keen**-tō*	20th	vigésimo *bee-**khe**-see-mō*
6th	sexto ***seks**-tō*	21st	vigésimo primero *bee-**khe**-see-mō pree-**may**-rō*
7th	séptimo ***sep**-tee-mō*	22nd	vigésimo segundo *bee-**khe**-see-mō say-**goon**-dō*
8th	octavo *ok-**ta**-bō*	23rd	vigésimo tercero *bee-**khe**-see-mō ter-**thay**-rō*
9th	noveno *nō-**bay**-nō*	30th	trigésimo *tree-**khe**-see-mō*
10th	décimo ***de**-thee-mō*	40th	cuadragésimo *kwa-dra-**khe**-see-mō*
11th	decimoprimero *de-the-mō-pree-**may**- rō*	50th	quincuagésimo *keen-kwa-**khe**-see-mō*
12th	decimosegundo *de-thee-mō-say-**goon**- dō*	100th	centésimo *then-**te**-see-mō*
13th	decimotercero *de-thee-mō-ter-**thay**- rō*	1,000th	milésimo *mee-**le**-see-mō*
14th	decimocuarto *de-thee-mō-**kwar**-tō*		
15th	decimoquinto *de-thee-mo-**keen**-tō*		

a half	medio ***may**-dyō*	a dozen	una docena *oo-na do-**thay**-na*
a quarter	un cuarto *oon **kwar**-tō*	half a dozen	media docena *may-dya do-**thay**-na*
a third	un tercio *oon **ter**-thyō*	5 times	cinco veces ***theeng**-kō be-thays*
10%	el diez por ciento *el dyeth por **thyen**-tō*	the last (one)	el último *el **ool**-tee-mō*

The Calendar

Sunday	domingo *do-**meeng**-gō*	**January**	enero *ay-**nay**-rō*
Monday	lunes *loo-nays*	**February**	febrero *fay-**bray**-rō*
Tuesday	martes *mar-tays*	**March**	marzo *mar-thō*
Wednesday	miércoles *myer-ko-lays*	**April**	abril *a-**breel***
Thursday	jueves *khway-bays*	**May**	mayo *ma-yō*
Friday	viernes *byer-nays*	**June**	junio *khoon-yō*
Saturday	sábado *sa-ba-dō*	**July**	julio *khool-yō*
on Friday	el viernes *el byer-nays*	**August**	agosto *a-**gos**-tō*
next Tuesday	el martes que viene *el mar-tays kay byay-nay*	**September**	setiembre *se-**tyem**-bray*
yesterday	ayer *a-**yer***	**October**	octubre *ok-**too**-bray*
today	hoy *oy*	**November**	noviembre *no-**byem**-bray*
tomorrow	mañana *man-ya-na*	**December**	diciembre *dee-**thyem**-bray*
spring	primavera *pree-ma-**bay**-ra*	**in June**	en junio *en **khoon**-yō*
summer	verano *bay-**ra**-nō*	**July 6th**	el seis de julio *el **se**-ees day **khool**-yō*
autumn (fall)	otoño *o-**ton**-yō*	**next week**	la semana próxima *la say-**ma**-na **prok**-see-ma*
winter	invierno *een-**byer**-nō*	**last month**	el mes pasado *el mes pa-**sa**-dō*
in spring	en la primavera *en la pree-ma-**bay**-ra*		
in summer	en el verano *en el bay-**ra**-nō*		

Public Holidays

New Year's Day – January 1st

Epiphany – January 6th

St. Joseph's Day – March 19th

Maundy Thursday

Good Friday

Corpus Christi

St. James' Day – July 25th

Assumption – August 15th

Hispanidad – October 12th

All Saints' Day – November 1st

Immaculate Conception – December 8th

Christmas Day – December 25th

The Alphabet

A	**como**	**Antonio**	**N**	**como**	**Navarra**
a	*kō-mō*	*an-tōn-yō*	*e̦-nay*	*kō-mō*	*na̦-ba̦-rra*
B	for	**Barcelona**	**Ñ**	for	**Noño**
bay		*bar-thay-lō-na*	*en-yay*		*nyo-nyō*
C		**Carmen**	**O**		**Oviedo**
thay		*kar-men*	*ō*		*ōb-yay-dō*
CH		**Chocolate**	**P**		**París**
chay		*cho-kō-la-tay*	*pay*		*pa-rees*
D		**Dolores**	**Q**		**Querido**
day		*do-lor-es*	*koo*		*kay-ree-dō*
E		**Enrique**	**R**		**Ramón**
ay		*en-ree-kay*	*e-ray*		*ra-mon*
F		**Francia**	**S**		**Sábado**
e-fay		*franth-ya*	*e-say*		*sa-ba-dō*
G		**Gerona**	**T**		**Tarragona**
khay		*khe-rō-na*	*tay*		*ta-rra-gō-na*
H		**Historia**	**U**		**Ulises**
a-chay		*ee-stōr-ya*	*oo*		*oo-lee-says*
I		**Inés**	**V**		**Valencia**
ee		*ee-nays*	*oo-bay*		*ba-len-thya*
J		**José**	**W**		**Washington**
khō-ta		*khō-say*	*oo-bay do-blay*		*wo-sheeng-ton*
K		**Kilo**	**X**		**Xiquena**
ka		*kee-lō*	*e-kees*		*khee-kay-na*
L		**Lorenzo**	**Y**		**Yegua**
e-lay		*lo-ren-thō*	*e gree-ay-ga*		*yeg-wa*
LL		**Llobregat**	**Z**		**Zaragoza**
el-yay		*lyō-bre-gat*	*thay-ta*		*tha-ra-gō-tha*
M		**Madrid**			
e-may		*ma-dreed*			

Abbreviations

C/	Calle (*Street*)
EE.UU.	Estados Unidos (*United States*)
M.I.T.	Ministerio de Información y Turismo (*Ministry of Information and Tourism*)
R.A.C.E.	Real Automóvil Club de España (*Spanish Automobile Club*)
RENFE	Red Nacional de Ferrocarriles Españoles (*Spanish Railways*)
R.N.E.	Radio Nacional de España (*Spanish Radio*)
S.A.	Socieded Anónima (*Limited Company*)
TVE	Televisión Española (*Spanish Television*)

Descriptions

First of all, a list of colours:

beige	beige *be-ees*	**mauve**	malva ***mal**-ba*
black	negro ***nay**-grō*	**orange**	naranja *na-**rang**-kha*
blue	azul *a-**thool***	**pink**	rosa ***rō**-sa*
brown	marrón *ma-**rron***	**purple**	morado *mō-**ra**-dō*
cream	crema ***kray**-ma*	**red**	rojo ***rō**-khō*
fawn	pardo claro ***par**-dō **kla**-rō*	**silver**	plateado *pla-tay-**a**-dō*
gold	dorado *dō-**ra**-dō*	**tan**	canela *ka-**nay**-la*
green	verde ***ber**-day*	**white**	blanco ***blang**-kō*
grey	gris *grees*	**yellow**	amarillo *a-ma-**reel**-yō*

and a few other handy adjectives:

bad	malo ***ma**-lō*	**fast**	rápido ***ra**-pee-dō*
beautiful	hermoso *er-**mō**-sō*	**good**	bueno ***bway**-nō*
big	grande ***gran**-day*	**little**	pequeño *pay-**kay**-nyō*
cheap	barato *ba-**ra**-tō*	**long**	largo ***lar**-gō*
cold	frío ***free**-ō*	**new**	nuevo ***nway**-bō*
dear	caro ***ka**-rō*	**old**	viejo ***byay**-khō*
difficult	difícil *dee-**fee**-theel*	**short**	corto ***kor**-tō*
easy	fácil ***fa**-theel*	**slow**	lento ***len**-tō*

Conversion Tables

In the tables for weight and length, you can treat the middle figure as either a metric or an imperial measurement. So to convert from pounds to kilos you look at the figure on the right, and for kilos to pounds you want the figure on the left.

lb		kg	litres	UK gallons	US gallons
2.2	1	0.45	5	1.1	1.3
4.4	2	0.91	10	2.2	2.6
6.6	3	1.4	15	3.3	3.9
8.8	4	1.8	20	4.4	5.2
11	5	2.2	25	5.5	6.5
13.2	6	2.7	30	6.6	7.8
15.4	7	3.2	35	7.7	9.1
17.6	8	3.6	40	8.8	10.4
19.8	9	4.1			
22	10	4.9			

inches		cm	feet		metres
0.39	1	2.54	3.3	1	0.3
0.79	2	5.08	6.6	2	0.61
1.18	3	7.62	9.9	3	0.91
1.57	4	10.6	13.1	4	1.22
1.97	5	12.7	16.4	5	1.52
2.36	6	15.2	19.7	6	1.83
2.76	7	17.8	23	7	2.13
3.15	8	20.3	26.2	8	2.44
3.54	9	22.9	29.5	9	2.74
3.9	10	25.4	32.9	10	3.05
4.3	11	27.9			
4.7	12	30.1			

Conversion Tables

kilometres	miles	centigrade	fahrenheit
10	6.2	0	32
20	12.4	5	41
30	18.6	10	50
40	24.9	15	59
50	31	17	63
60	37.3	20	68
70	43.5	22	72
80	49.7	24	75
90	56	26	79
100	62	28	82
110	68.3	30	86
120	74.6	35	95
130	81	37	98.4
140	87	38	100
150	93.2	40	104
160	100	50	122
200	124	100	212
300	186		
500	310		

Tyre Pressures

lb/sq in	15	18	20	22	24	26	28	30	33	35
kg/sq cm	1.1	1.3	1.4	1.5	1.7	1.8	2	2.1	2.3	2.5

Exchange Rates

£1 =	$1 =
50 pesetas =	1,000 pesetas =
100 pesetas =	2,000 pesetas =
250 pesetas =	5,000 pesetas =
500 pesetas =	10,000 pesetas =

Place-names

Alcalá de	*al-ka-**la** day*	**Córdoba**	***kor**-dō-ba*
Henares	*ay-**na**-rays*	**Coruña**	*ko-**roon**-ya*
Algeciras	*al-khay-**thee**-ras*	**Estartit**	*es-tar-**teet***
Alicante	*a-lee-**kan**-tay*	**Estepona**	*es-tay-**po**-na*
Almería	*al-may-**ree**-a*	**Figueras**	*fee-**gay**-ras*
Ampurias	*am-**poor**-yas*	**Fuengirola**	*fwen-khee-**rō**-la*
Andújar	*an-**doo**-khar*	**Gerona**	*khay-**rō**-na*
Antequera	*an-tay-**kay**-ra*	**Gibraltar**	*khee-bral-**tar***
Aranjuez	*a-rang-**khweth***	**Granada**	*gra-**na**-da*
Arcos de la	*ar-kōs day la*	**Guadeloupe**	*gwa-day-**loo**-pay*
Frontera	*fron-**tay**-ra*	**Guadix**	***gwa**-deeks*
Astorga	*as-**tor**-ga*	**Huelva**	***wel**-ba*
Avila	***a**-bee-la*	**Ibiza**	*ee-**bee**-tha*
Badajoz	*ba-da-**khoth***	**Illetas**	*eel-**yay**-tas*
Baeza	*ba-**ay**-tha*	**Jaca**	***kha**-ka*
Bailén	*ba-ee-**len***	**Jaén**	*kha-**en***
Bañolas	*ban-**yō**-las*	Jerez de la	*khe-**reth** day la*
Barcelona	*bar-thay-**lō**-na*	Frontera	*fron-**tay**-ra*
Bilbao	*beel-**ba**-ō*	**León**	*lay-**on***
Blanes	***bla**-nays*	**Lloret de Mar**	*lyo-**ret** day mar*
Burgos	***boor**-gōs*	**Madrid**	*ma-**dreed***
Cabrera	*ka-**bray**-ra*	**Málaga**	***ma**-la-ga*
Cáceres	***ka**-thay-rays*	**Manacor**	*ma-na-**kor***
Cadaqués	*ka-da-**kays***	**Martos**	***mar**-tos*
Cádiz	***ka**-deeth*	**Mérida**	***me**-ree-da*
Cala Bona	***ka**-la **bō**-na*	**Montilla**	*mon-**teel**-ya*
Calella	*ka-**lel**-ya*	**Murcia**	***moor**-thya*
Camp de Mar	*kamp day **mar***	**Nerja**	***ner**-kha*
Camprodón	*kam-prō-**don***	**Olot**	*o-**lot***
Cartagena	*kar-ta-**khay**-na*	**Orense**	*o-**ren**-say*
Ciudad	*thyoo-**dad** ro-**dree**-gō*	**Oviedo**	*ob-**yay**-dō*
Rodrigo		**Paguera**	*pa-**gay**-ra*

Place-names

Palamos	*pa-la-mōs*	Sevilla	*say-beel-ya*
Palencia	*pa-len-thya*	Sitges	*seet-chays*
Palma de	*pal-ma day*	Soller	*sol-yer*
Mallorca	*mal-yor-ka*	Soria	*sor-ya*
Palma Nova	*pal-ma nō-ba*	Tarifa	*ta-ree-fa*
Pamplona	*pam-plō-na*	Tarragona	*ta-rra-gō-na*
Perelada	*pay-ray-la-da*	Teruel	*ter-wel*
Puerto de	*pwer-tō day san-ta*	Toledo	*to-lay-dō*
Santa	*ma-ree-a*	Torre-	*to-rray-mo-lee-nōs*
María		molinos	
Ribadeo	*ree-ba-day-ō*	Tossa de Mar	*to-sa day mar*
Ripoll	*ree-poly'*	Trujillo	*troo-kheel-yō*
Ronda	*ron-da*	Tudela	*too-day-la*
Rosas	*rō-sas*	Úbeda	*oo-bay-da*
Salamanca	*sa-la-mang-ka*	Ullastret	*ool-yas-tret*
San Felíu de	*san fay-lee-oo*	Utrera	*oo-tray-ra*
Guixols	*day gee-shols*	Valencia	*ba-len-thya*
Sanlúcar de	*san-loo-kar day*	Valladolid	*bal-ya-do-leed*
Barrameda	*ba-rra-may-da*	Valldemosa	*baly'-day-mō-sa*
San Sebastián	*san say-bas-tyan*	Vitoria	*bee-tōr-ya*
Santander	*san-tan-der*	Zamora	*tha-mō-ra*
Santiago	*san-tya-gō*	Zaragoza	*tha-ra-gō-tha*
Segovia	*say-gōv-ya*		

Signs & Notices

Abierto	Open
Acceso a los andenes	This way to the trains
Aduana	Customs
Alto	Stop
Ascensor	Lift (elevator)
Caballeros	Gentlemen
Caja (*in shop*)	Pay here
(*in bank etc*)	Cash desk
Cerrado	Closed
Completo	Full
Consigna	Left Luggage (baggage room)
Damas	Ladies
Degustación	Sampling (*of wine etc*)
Despacio	Slow
Desviación	Detour
Empuje	Push
Entrada	Way in
Entrada Libre	No obligation to buy
Estacionamiento prohibido	No parking
Libre	Vacant
No funciona	Out of order
No tocar / **No toquen, por favor**	Do not touch

Signs & Notices

Ocupado	–	Engaged
Pase sin llamar	–	Walk in, no need to knock
Peligro	–	Danger
Pinta	–	Wet Paint
Policía	–	Police
Privada	–	Private
Prohibida le entrada **Prohibido el paso**	–	No entry
Prohibido bañarse	–	No bathing
Prohibido fumar	–	No smoking
Prohibido pisar la hierba	–	Keep off the grass
Rebajas	–	Sale
Salida	–	Exit
Señoras	–	Ladies
Servicio incluido	–	Service included
Servicio no incluido	–	Service not included
Servicios	–	Toilets
Se prohibe	–	see 'prohibido'
Silencio	–	Silence
Teléfono	–	Telephone
Tirad	–	Pull

Index

Index

Index

Index